D0897638

NORMAN MAILER
A CRITICAL STUDY

NORMAN MAILER

A CRITICAL STUDY

JEAN RADFORD

First published 1975 by
THE MACMILLAN PRESS LTD
London and Basingstoke
Associated companies in New York
Dublin Melbourne Johannesburg and Madras

SBN 333 17409 7

Photoset and printed
in Great Britain by
REDWOOD BURN LIMITED
Trowbridge & Esher

for Luke

Contents

Acknowledgements

The author and publishers wish to thank the following for permission to use the extracts from Norman Mailer's works quoted in this study:

Jonathan Cape Ltd for *Barbary Shore; Commentary* for Richard Poirier's review, 'Morbid-Mindedness', of Norman Mailer's *An American Dream*, from *Commentary* (June 1965); Thomas Y. Crowell Co. Inc. for *Miami and the Siege of Chicago*, Copyright © 1968 by Norman Mailer; Andre Deutsch Ltd for *Advertisements for Myself, The Presidential Papers, An American Dream, Cannibals and Christians, The Naked and the Dead,* and *The Deer Park*; George Weidenfeld & Nicolson Ltd. for *The Prisoner of Sex, Miami and the Siege of Chicago, The Armies of the Night,* and *Why Are We in Vietnam?*

Extracts from the following works are reprinted by permission of the author and the author's agents, Scott Meredith Literary Agency, Inc., 580 Fifth Avenue, New York, New York 10036: *The Naked and the Dead, Barbary Shore, An American Dream, Cannibals and Christians, The Armies of the Night, Miami and the Siege of Chicago, The Prisoner of Sex, St. George and The Godfather, Marilyn, The Deer Park, Why Are We in Vietnam?, The Presidential Papers* and *Advertisements for Myself.*

Introduction

Now, after the publication of *Marilyn* in 1973, seems to me a good time to attempt a critical study of Mailer's work. A good time because the books which he has written since *The Armies of the Night* represent, I think, a repetition, a recapitulation of earlier efforts and thus make it an opportune moment to consider his past achievements.

In this study I have concentrated on the period from 1948 to 1968, although I have also referred to *A Fire on the Moon* (1970), *The Prisoner of Sex* (1971), *St. George and the Godfather* (1972), and *Marilyn* (1973) in discussing the later work. These latest books suggest that Mailer has reached a state of intellectual and stylistic crisis where he is trapped in the contradictions and limitations of the vision which first emerged in 'The White Negro' essay in 1957, and which with extensions and modifications has been the basis of his subsequent work. I see *The Armies of the Night* as the real culmination point in this process: as a watershed in the muted autobiography of Norman Mailer which runs throughout his *oeuvre*, as an essay at the big novel about America which it has been his ambition to write for the last fifteen years, and as a reaffirmation of the novel as a form and a philosophical justification of the 'novelistic' approach to experience.

Throughout his development Mailer seems to have found 'fictionality' less and less easy to maintain. Perhaps not since his first novel where he successfully transformed his experience with the 112th Cavalry in the Pacific during World War II, into a fictional treatment of war, has he succeeded in creating or sustaining a fictional construct which is autonomous in the traditional way. In *Barbary Shore* the fictional world of the Brooklyn boarding-house and its inhabitants collapses into a chapter of political speech, and the fiction never becomes 'real' again. In

1

The Deer Park he creates a convincing imaginative situation with Eitel at its centre, but, as the unevenness of the novel suggests, Mailer is less interested in this than in developing aspects for which he has as yet no adequate novelistic technique. At this point in his literary career, Mailer seemed unable to create fiction which would support the idiosyncratic and urgent nature of his vision, and his voice and preoccupations are continually breaking into his imaginative work. Having begun in these early novels by experimenting with the ideas and techniques of various American and European traditions, he began in the mid-fifties to discard these, and to search for a new voice – a new and more 'muscular' style in which to express his changing conception of the writer, his new kind of radicalism and what I have called his 'crisis-philosophy'. *Advertisements for Myself* both documents and embodies this process of change, and I have treated it as representative of the stylistic and ideological break in his development, as a point of rupture (which in fact was a process taking several years) from his early achievements.

In following this interpretation, I have not attempted to situate Mailer in relation to other contemporary American writers, nor to make any general assessment of his relation to the contemporary social and intellectual movements which figure so largely in his writing. For although a more contextual treatment may ultimately prove the best way of assessing the literary significance of this particular writer, it falls outside my reach and would perhaps, at this moment of his career, be premature. Instead I have tried to offer fairly close readings of the different books – looking at the language, imagery and ideas of the individual texts – under four main aspects. The first chapter is an attempt to trace the changes in Mailer's conception of man and man's potential through an examination of the heroes of each of his novels and some of his essays. His view of human nature, which moves from the somewhat determinist perspective of *The Naked and the Dead* to a more existentialist view of man as a 'collection of possibilities' in his middle and later works, is clearly visible in the characterisation; I have tried to identify three main heroic types: the tragic liberal hero of the Hearn, McLeod, Eitel type; the existentialist hipster exemplified in Faye, the 'White Negro', Rojack and DJ; and the Mailer creations of his later period which are very close to Mailer's hipsters but form a distinctive and separate group in themselves. I have also attempted to trace the way in which certain ideas persist – like that about the dual nature of man as 'beast' and 'seer' – through the patterns of imagery.

Chapter 2 is a critical description of the political and ideological development in his work, charting the movement from the Marxist influence apparent in *The Naked and the Dead* and the Trotskyist perspective in *Barbary Shore*, through to an anarchist opposition to the centralised state and Mailer's fears of 'totalitarianism'. This anti-totalitarianism and the hopes for resistance and opposition which he centres in the individual consciousness are what chiefly characterise the political writings of *The Presidential Papers* and *Cannibals and Christians*. Although later in the sixties, notably in *The Armies of the Night*, Mailer is able to find common ground with sections of the American New Left on the basis of a shared concern with subjectivity and anti-authoritarianism, I have tried to suggest the contradictions and limitations of his new political definition of himself as a 'Left Conservative'.[1]

After a central chapter on Mailer's stylistics, I have gone on to discuss his fictional treatment of women and his ideas about sexuality and instinctivism generally. As with his philosophical and political development, I find that his attitudes to women undergo considerable changes in the mid-fifties, around the time of *The Deer Park* and *Advertisements for Myself*. By examining the treatment of sexuality in each of the books, I have attempted to suggest the relation between these attitudes and his social and political outlook generally. Recent criticisms of his work as 'reactionary' or even 'counter-revolutionary' in terms of sexual politics, have failed to take sufficient account of two things; first, that Mailer has always used sexual relations in a highly stylised, rather Lawrentian way, to symbolise his view of *social* relations, and secondly, that there are considerable differences in his early treatment of women and his later. In the writing following *Advertisements for Myself* women and femininity seem to have replaced the homosexuals of the earliest novels, as symbols of negativity and I have argued that this development is a logical outcome of his 'organicist' opposition to totalitarianism.

In this study I have deliberately chosen to discuss certain thematic and political trends in Mailer's work before considering his style in the belief that these trends are crucial to an understanding of his artistic progress, and illuminate stylistic changes which might appear arbitrary from a purely literary standpoint. As Mailer commented in *Advertisements for Myself*,

> The difficulty for most people who are at all interested in my work is that I started as one kind of writer, and I've been evolving into another kind of writer.[2]

Since the changes themselves are fairly obvious, the difficulty it seems to me, is rather to understand the nature and object of Mailer's changing style and to relate his stylistic evolution to the development of his political and philosophical concerns. Despite the fact that he is, as both *Advertisements for Myself* and *The Armies of the Night* reveal, a highly self-conscious writer and craftsman, he has never been primarily interested in formal or aesthetic questions but has seen style as inseparable from what he calls 'vision'. (See his comment on Faulkner's influence on him in *Advertisements for Myself*.*) I have not paid too much attention to questions of *genre*, since his use of different *genres* and styles all seem to me to relate to his idea of himself as a writer; the fact that he has not so far committed himself to a particular prose style or aesthetic form is not simply a literary decision but stems from his large and intensely moral view of the writer's social function.

The writer, and particularly the novelist, in Mailer's view, has the responsibility not merely of making imaginative constructions from reality as he sees it, but of changing that reality by offering a sufficiently cogent vision of present and future possibilities in the world. His assessment of writers is always in terms of how far they do this, whether they produce 'work which would clarify a nation's vision of itself'.[3] He finds fault with Faulkner and Hemingway, whom he sees as the best twentieth-century American writers, because they fall short of this task:

> Their vision was partial, determinedly so, they saw that as the first condition for trying to be great – that one must not try to save. Not souls, and not the nation.[4]

---

* '. . . it seems obvious that the influence was there. And profoundly. Faulkner's style – which is to say, his vision – was to haunt my later themes like the ghost of some undiscovered mansion in my mind.' (pp. 78–9)

Mailer's own priorities are different; eschewing the pursuit of 'partial' greatness or stylistic excellence in favour of the messianic task of 'saving' the world, his style in each book adapts itself to the task in hand – as he sees it. As early as 1959, in *Advertisements for Myself*, Mailer admitted the extent of his literary ambitions which have in my opinion, been the source of both the strengths and weaknesses in his writing:

> [to] . . . settle for nothing less than making a revolution in the consciousness of our time. Whether rightly or wrongly, it is then obvious that I would go so far as to think it is my present and future work which will have the deepest influence of any work being done by an American novelist in these years.[5]

This objective, although modified somewhat in his later work, is the constant throughout the stylistic fluctuations. All through his literary development since *The Naked and the Dead*, in his experiments with the novel form, the short story, essay, journalism, interview, biography, and poetry and drama, one can discern the search for a style tuned to the consciousness of his time, the search for a voice big enough to carry the vision which would 'clarify a nation'.

1 'The Beast and the Seer': Mailer's Search for a Hero

In the author's eyes, The Naked and the Dead is not a realistic documentary; it is rather a 'symbolic' book, of which the basic theme is the conflict between the beast and the seer in man. The number of events experienced by the one platoon couldn't possible have happened to any one army platoon in the war, but represent a composite view of the Pacific War. The mountain the platoon attempts to climb represents death and man's creative urge, fate and man's desire to conquer the elements – all kinds of things that you'd never dream of separating and stating so baldly.

Taking the title and starting-point of this chapter from Mailer's comment in *Current Biography* (1948) that 'the basic theme is the conflict between the beast and the seer in man,' I want to discuss *The Naked and the Dead* in this light and establish that *underlying* the political elements in his work there is a continuous philosophical debate about the nature of man – his needs, drives and heroic potential. The conflict between Hearn and Cummings represents a clash about political ideology which constitutes one of the most thoroughgoing and sophisticated discussions of political issues to be found in any war novel, but beyond the clash about the political (the merits and demerits of different social systems) are the more fundamental questions posed in the diary of the dead Japanese officer:

I ask myself – WHY? I am born, I am to die. WHY? WHY? What is the meaning?[1]

In the characters not only of Hearn and Cummings, Croft and Valsen but each of the soldiers in the platoon, Mailer uses the war situation to explore questions of man's basic drives and

7

psychic needs. Each man is forced to confront the fact of death and is stripped 'naked' by the experience – forced to confront the most basic questions about man's existence, his relation to God, the natural world and other men. He is forced to do this in the context of an 'unheroic' war; to define himself under conditions of extreme physical exhaustion and monotonous hardship.

Cummings believes that beyond the desire to survive and the sexual urge, instincts which men share with other animals, man's primary drive (*qua* man) is toward the achievement of power over other men and the natural world. His belief in the 'fear-ladder' stems directly from this view of man; if man's essential nature is to struggle for power, then his relation with other men is governed by the power principle and other considerations like those suggested by Hearn ('the continual occurrence and reforming of certain great ethical ideas') are betrayals of human nature. His political convictions follow logically from this position as he himself points out to Robert Hearn:

> The concept of Fascism, far sounder than communism if you consider it, for it's grounded firmly in men's actual natures, merely started in the wrong country . . .[2]

Mailer uses the Time Machine device to present the emotional and psychological factors in Cummings' childhood, military school training which in part determined this intellectual position. But it was whilst serving as an officer in the First World War that he first experiences his own desire for power:

> To command all that. He is choked with the intensity of his emotion, the rage, the exaltation, the undefined and mighty hunger.[3]

His relationships, in marriage and with other officers, offer no alternative to this hunger for power; the contradictory impulses, as in the episode in Rome, are firmly suppressed. He accepts the estrangement from other men that the search for individual power necessarily imposes and rejects any momentary regrets:

> Always, he had to be alone, he had chosen it that way, and he

would not renege now, nor did he want to. The best things, the things worth doing in the last analysis, had to be done alone. The moments like these, the passing doubts, were the temptations that caught you if you were not careful. Cummings stared at the vast dark bulk of Mount Anaka, visible in the darkness as a deeper shadow, a greater mass than the sky above it . . . There's an affinity, he told himself. If one wanted to get mystical about it, the mountain and he understood each other. Both of them, from necessity, were bleak and alone, commanding the heights.[4]

Cummings recognises the undefined and mighty hunger in himself as the 'largest vision that has ever entered his soul'[5] and accepts it not merely as his own driving force but as that of all men. He dedicates himself – and this dedication is the heroic element in his character – both personally and politically to the 'power morality'.

Croft's heroic potential, free from the suggestion of sublimated homosexuality, emerges more strongly than that of Cummings – no one equals Croft for effective leadership and active courage. With no developed political theories, he represents another aspect of the 'seer' in man and has his own 'vistas of. . . omnipotence'.[6] He enjoys his power of command over the men in the platoon and accepts their fear and hatred as the inevitable corollary of that leadership and, unlike Cummings, experiences no desire or regret for other kinds of relationships. He compensates for a closeness with other men by his feeling for nature and like Cummings feels a special affinity with Mount Anaka:

Again, he felt a crude ecstasy. He could not have given the reason, but the mountain tormented him, beckoned him, held an answer to something he wanted.[7]

Croft is, as Polack says of him, an idealist, and his attempt to reach the peak of the mountain shows a degree of courage and tenacity which are in a sense heroic because he attempts to 'conquer the elements' with his willpower. It is this violent assertion of *will* which links Croft to some of Mailer's later hero-figures.

Seeing other men in these terms (in their own image), both

Croft and Cummings feel only contempt for those who cannot or lack the *will* to commit themselves to the power-struggle. Croft's reaction to Red's rebelliousness is contemptuous dismissal:

> It was always the men who never got anywhere who did the bitching.[8]

and significantly he dislikes Hearn's desire to be friendly with the platoon, to 'buddy' with the men.

Although articulated in a different way, Cummings is disappointed with Hearn for similar reasons. In the discussion shortly before he demonstrates to Hearn the personal application of the fear-ladder (by forcing him to pick up the cigarette butt on pain of court-martial), Cummings asks Hearn what he takes 'man's deepest urge to be'.[9] When Hearn flippantly suggests it is the sexual urge, he dismisses men's relations with women as merely 'a yardstick among other gauges by which to measure superiority' and in the conversation which follows sets out the psychological justification for the 'power morality' – for romantic fascism:

> 'The truth of it is that from man's very inception there has been one great vision, blurred first by the exigencies and cruelties of nature, and then, as nature began to be conquered, by the second great cloak – economic fear and economic striving . . . There's that popular misconception of man as something between a brute and an angel. Actually man is in transit between brute and God.'
>
> 'Man's deepest urge is omnipotence?'
>
> 'Yes. It's not religion, that's obvious, it's not love, it's not spirituality, those are all sops along the way, benefits we devise for ourselves when the limitations of our existence turn us away from the other great dream. To achieve God. When we come kicking into the world, we *are* God, the universe is the limit of our senses. And when we get older, when we discover the universe is not us, it's the deepest trauma of our existence.'
>
> Hearn fingered his collar. 'I'd say *your* deepest urge is omnipotence, that's all.'
>
> 'And yours too, whether you'll admit it or not.'[10]

The strength of Cummings' political position seemingly is that it is consistent with his view of human nature, which as Hearn points out in their argument, is based on his, Cummings' nature. Hearn's weakness is twofold: he neither challenges the terms of Cummings's argument (by pointing out that man is not 'essentially' either power-seeking or not – that the 'dream' may have a social rather than a psychological explanation) nor offers a consistent humanist view of human nature. Therefore once he is forced to recognise Cummings' view of man in *himself*, he is thrown back into self-denigration and theoretical impotence. Shortly before his death, he recognises something of his predicament:

> Beyond Cummings, deeper now, was his own desire to lead the platoon. It had grown, ignited suddenly, become one of the most satisfying things he had ever done. He could understand Croft's staring at the mountain through the fieldglasses, or killing the bird. When he searched himself he was just another Croft[11]

The reasons for Hearn's similarities to Croft and Cummings (but without their 'visionary' qualities) are presented in the Time Machine, 'The Addled Womb'. His political liberalism fails to oppose Cummings' 'peculiarly American' fascism in their discussions, but it also fails at the practical level, in his relations with other men. The 'great ethical ideas' remain abstractions and there is nothing to correspond to them in Hearn's personal practice. His distrust of emotional involvement leaves him as isolated as Croft and Cummings, but without their ability to relate to men as leaders he is in fact left only with his own disengaged intelligence:

> To lose his inviolate freedom was to become involved again in all the wants and sores that caught up everybody about him.[12]

Both Hearn and Valsen 'get by on style'[13], a style without content, a vague ideal of personal integrity and a lack of commitment in personal relations, and Mailer exposes the weakness of both in their parallel and symbolic defeat at the hands of Cummings and Croft. Despite their different positive qualities both men fail to achieve heroic stature and fail to maintain even their idea of themselves. Mailer stresses in both characterisations their failure to accept involvement with others, repeatedly describing their withdrawal from social bonds. Valsen leaves the woman and child with whom he has lived fairly happily for several years for the excitement of being on the move and drinking through his regrets, and this pattern continues in his relationships with other enlisted men in the platoon. He represses moments of sympathy and solidarity in order to retain his independence:

> Deep inside him he was feeling a trace of sympathy for Goldstein but he smothered it. 'A man ain't worth a damn if he can't even take care of himself,' Red muttered.[14]

He refuses greater closeness with Gallagher, Roth and Wyman at different times on the grounds that 'he allowed himself to like no-one so well that it would hurt if he was lost.'[15] Neither Hearn nor Valsen, the intellectual rebel and the 'natural' rebel, represents an alternative to the exponents of the power morality and neither offers a 'vision' of other heroic possibilities; it is Goldstein and Ridges, the two who most fully accept the 'burdens' of their interdependence, who offer us a glimpse of a quite different kind of heroic endeavour.

The narrative unfolds through the invasion of Anopopei, the deadlocked campaign, the reconnaissance expedition behind enemy lines, the unforeseen Japanese collapse and finally the mopping-up operations and a return to ironic normality; the theme of the beast and the seer in man is developed both within this narrative pattern and in the densely patterned imagery. The Japanese, the jungle and the weather are the determining conditions of the platoon's existence and the "seers" are those who struggle most heroically against these forces – those who assert their willpower in opposition to these forces. Others, who succumb to the force of nature or to another's will, are the unheroic majority who yield to the merely animal desire to survive at all costs. This point is made insistently in the comparison of the men with ants, insects, cattle and other forms of animal life; in the opening section the idea is first introduced in the reference to Pavlov's experiments with dogs[16] and then in the image of the advancing army as 'a nest of ants'.[17] Wherever human activity becomes mechanical, as in the physically heroic movement of the machine guns, it becomes dehumanised, robbed of heroic element, and this point is made in the images of 'darkness', 'blindness' and animality:

> Then darkness swirled about them again, and they ground the guns forward blindly, a line of ants dragging their burden back to their hole.[18]

In battle, killing becomes 'as easy as stepping on an insect';[19] even the relief of a temporary encampment is described in terms of comfort at the animal level:

> They were dogs in their own kennel now.[20]

This presentation of the enlisted men and their mammoth exertions is itself one of the ideological points the novel makes about American involvement in the Second World War: the total alienation of the enlisted men from the war at any level other than their physical participation. Almost no one in the platoon (and virtually every personality type from almost every geographical area in America is represented) has any larger understanding of the war, any informing ideal. It is an unheroic war. The individual virtues possessed by the men – Martinez' pride in his abilities as a scout and soldier, Ridges' and Goldstein's affection and concern for their families, even Toglio's childish patriotism – gain little recognition or importance in the functioning of the group. In this sense the platoon is a microcosm of the army as a whole, and the promotion of Stanley can be seen as an illustration of Cummings' dictum about the army. The destructiveness of this kind of organisation is reflected in the deterioration of almost every man: in the increase in Croft's sadism (shown in the incident with the Japanese soldiers), the growing isolation and demoralisation of Valsen, the embitterment of Roth and Goldstein from the others' anti-semitism and the brutalisation of Martinez (which comes to a climax when he smashes a corpse's mouth to obtain the gold teeth). In this last incident particularly, Mailer suggests that outcome to which the continual denial of their common humanity within the platoon points. In desecrating the dead of his own species, man is shedding his own identification as a human being, breaking all civilised (socially constructed) taboos and reverting to a level beyond that of 'beast'.

Goldstein and Ridges, of the men in the platoon, are the two who manage to resist the force of their circumstances, and who struggle to maintain ideas that go beyond the survival principle. These two, in resisting the 'temptation'[21] to put their own interests and safety before all else take a stand, however limited, against what Mailer was later to call 'barbarism'. The source of their resistance stems, in both cases, from their strong if ill-defined religious beliefs. Like Croft, both are keenly responsive to nature, but where Croft sees it as an opponent to be struggled with and conquered, Goldstein and Ridges exhibit an acceptance and reverence for nature of a pre-technological, religious view of the world. Watching the storm that uproots their tents, Goldstein feels 'a deep excitement as if he were witnessing creation'[22], and Ridges similarly

> felt the throbbing of the jungle as a part of himself, the earth, which had turned to a golden mud, seemed alive to him.[23]

This generalised, unsophisticated religious feeling also provides the basis for their attitudes to their fellow men, typified by Ridges' reaction to Goldstein:

> He had helped Goldstein pound in the stakes because you helped your neighbour when he asked for it, and Ridges had decided the man you bunked with, even if he was a stranger, was still your neighbour.[24]

In the counterpointed descriptions of the two expeditions (the Mount Anaka climbers and those who carry Wilson on a litter to the beach), Mailer accentuates the symbolic nature of 'the litter-bearers'[25] journey by describing it in terms of a religious trial. Goldstein and Ridges continue long after there is any hope of saving Wilson's life to the point where their efforts are solely in order to get the dead body to the seashore. Similarly, Croft's group makes its maximum exertions to scale the mountain after an inserted passage detailing the break through the Toyaku line and the virtual defeat of the Japanese. Mailer thus makes it clear that both journeys have become, objectively, futile. This, in part, is their significance on the narrative level, but both journeys are given a ritualistic significance by the language in which they are presented. The enormity of the men's physical efforts is insisted on at a very concrete level, but the biblical rhythms and language used to convey the experience of the litter-bearers contrasts sharply with the emphasis on the physical agonies of Croft's party.

The litter-bearers are 'men walking through flame',[26] they carry Wilson's body 'as if they were wrestling with a stone'.[27] They endure not merely their exhaustion but also the temptation to give him water (which would kill him) and to go on without him as he, deliriously, begs them to do:

Each of them was fighting his private battle.[28]

When Stanley and Brown give up the struggle, Goldstein and Ridges decide to go on and Wilson becomes the embodiment of man's 'load',[29] his 'burden',[30] and their journey becomes 'all existence'.[31] For Goldstein, 'after an eternity of wrestling Wilson's body through an empty and alien land'[32], carrying Wilson becomes a symbol for the burden of his own life and his Jewishness, equivalent to the 'heart' as 'Israel is the heart of all nations.'[33] When the body is finally lost, Ridges the Christian fundamentalist makes a similar identification between his own everyday struggle to live and the struggle to carry Wilson:

what counted was that he had carried this burden through such distances of space and time, and it had washed away in the end. All his life he had laboured without repayment; his grandfather and his father and he had struggled with bleak crops and unending poverty . . .[34]

Stanley and Brown are defined by the army and confirm Cummings' view of human nature, whereas Goldstein and Ridges define themselves *against* the conditions and values of the army and, it is implied, of their time. In their struggles they uphold the distinction between man and beast and achieve a mutual recognition and solidarity which Mailer suggests is valuable despite their 'humiliating failure'[35] and their lack of the kind of active heroism that Croft embodies. This basic achievement is underlined in the scene on the beach where Goldstein, after a struggle with himself, shares his water-bottle with Ridges; and this modest achievement-in-failure is balanced against Croft's heroic failure to realise himself in 'conquering the elements'. Both journeys are treated symbolically as essays in the heroic, as different aspects of 'seer' in man but Goldstein and Ridges' heroism is not something Mailer returns to in his later search for heroic models and the reasons lie, possibly, in Goldstein's comment on his new 'goy friend':

> Ridges was a good man. There was something enduring about him. The salt of the earth, Goldstein told himself.[36]

The 'goodness' of Goldstein and Ridges, like their religious views of the world, is anachronistic in a world containing Cummings and Croft. They possess the passive 'goodness' which endures in such a world but does not change it, and in his novels after *The Naked and the Dead* Mailer's search is for a hero who has the force to change the world. It is in fact Croft* who stands as the prototype of Marion Faye, 'The White Negro' and Rojack – Mailer's later heroes.

In Mailer's second novel, *Barbary Shore* (1951), the humanistic values of Goldstein and Ridges are noticeably absent. Hollingsworth the anti-hero embodies some of the qualities of Croft and Cummings along with the role and sensibilities of Major Dalleson, while McLeod and Lovett represent the heroic principle betrayed and in defeat. None of the characters in *Barbary Shore* is an even partial expression of Mailer's ideal heroism which appears to exist only in the future, embodied in 'the little object'. Nevertheless, the 'conflict between the beast and the seer in man' is again expressed in images of blindness, darkness and animality and at the discursive level in the speeches of McLeod, revealing the thematic continuities between *Barbary Shore* and *The Naked and the Dead*. Mailer's attempt, as he describes it in *Advertisements for Myself*, was 'to find some amalgam of my new experience and the larger horror of the world which might be preparing to destroy itself'.[37] The shift from wartime realism to peacetime allegory is accompanied by a shift in emphasis from characterisation to ideology, and the 'larger horror' of the post-war world is worked out in the interaction of the half dozen inmates of a Brooklyn boarding-house.

Unlike *The Naked and the Dead* with its numerous characters

* As Mailer comments in *The Presidential Papers* (p. 149): 'Beneath the ideology in *The Naked and the Dead* was an obsession with violence. The characters for whom I had most secret admiration, like Croft, were violent people.'

realistically presented, the sextet of three male and three female characters exist as personified ideas: Lannie Madison, Guinivere and Monina exhibit the pathological, debased and 'monistic' nature of American civilisation and their counterparts, Lovett, Hollingsworth and McLeod, reflect the causes of this condition as the females represent the effects. The alliance of Guinivere and Hollingsworth at the end of the novel, and their departure 'To the ends of the earth. To Barbary'[38] represent Mailer's apocalyptic view of the world at present. The 'little object' is in Lovett's possession and may re-emerge in the future but for the moment it has like Lovett 'gone underground' in a world given over to the marriage of the totalitarian and the barbaric:

> But for the present the storm approaches its thunderhead, and it is apparent that the boat drifts ever closer to shore. So the blind will lead the blind, and the deaf shout warnings to one another until their voices are lost.[39]

The 'blind' in *Barbary Shore* as in *The Naked and the Dead* are those without the vision that makes man superior to the animal world, exemplified by Hollingsworth and Guinivere. The vessel of civilisation, in the same metaphor, is drifting helplessly down upon Barbary Shore and although voices (like those of Lovett and McLeod) shout their warnings, they are lost in the 'shrieking and caterwauling of animals washed over the dam'.[40] The need clearly, in the terms of the allegory, is for seers, visionaries of sufficient heroic stature to lead men back from the dam, to oppose the drift and tendency of their time. The same point is made by McLeod, in his view of the future:

> It depends upon the potentiality of the human, and that is an open question, impossible to determine philosophically. Well may it be that men in sufficient numbers and with sufficient passion and consciousness to create such a world will never exist. If they do not, then the human condition is incapable of alleviation, and we can only witness for a century at least and perhaps for ever the disappearance of all we have created[41]

Both McLeod's pessimism and his prescription – for men 'with sufficient passion and consciousness' – are central to the novel.

In the past, possessed of both 'passion and consciousness', McLeod attempted, with others, the task he outlines to Lovett. His failure and the reasons for his failure are presented in the confession-interrogation sessions with Hollingsworth, where with Lannie Madison and Lovett for witnesses, the moral history of socialism is reviewed. This history is used to illustrate the reasons why Lovett, McLeod's apprentice, turns aside from political movements and suggests as well why Mailer in his later work created heroes outside any form of organised politics.

McLeod is a revolutionary socialist who worked for the Communist Party for nineteen years, mainly in Europe, and became known during this period as 'the Hangman of the Left'. After what he calls 'nineteen years with the wrong woman'[42] and the signing of the Nazi–Soviet pact, he leaves and returns to the US to work for the State Department. After a year of this he leaves and works at various jobs under the name of William McLeod. Traced by the FBI who wish to recover the mysterious 'little object', he agrees to undergo interrogation by the agent Hollingsworth. It is during these interrogation sessions that his past actions are reconstructed, and the historical and political forces which defeated him (and the Revolution) are presented. His room in the boarding-house (each room is used to symbolise the character of its occupant) resembles a cell; he is by nature an ascetic and by cast of mind disciplined and rational. He is not betrayed by appetite nor love of power but by the very professionalism he brings to his task. Mailer follows the Trotskyist interpretation that the revolution was betrayed by the bureaucratism of the Stalinists in dealing with the economic crises following the revolution, and McLeod's failure is situated in this analysis; the theorist and revolutionary becomes an instrument of the Stalinist State and is active throughout the purges and work camps of the thirties. His attempts to stifle his own misgivings in more rigid orthodoxy and instrumentality culminate in the murder of a former comrade who openly expresses McLeod's doubts. The attempt of the Party bureaucrat to return to theoretical work is cut short by the appearance of Hollingsworth and the interrogation. The bureaucrat of monopoly capitalism then faces the former bureaucrat of 'State capitalism' and the parallel is recognised by McLeod himself:

the truth is that there are deep compacts between Leroy and myself, you might almost say we are sympathetic to each other.[43]

At this point the indictment is complete; the betrayal of the revolutionary ideals puts McLeod on a level with Hollingsworth, and the man who makes himself an instrument of the State (whether Capitalist or Socialist) is a renegade as a hero. Like Eitel in *The Deer Park*, McLeod serves as an example to younger men, and their intense awareness of their own defeat enables them to act as spokesmen for the heroic principle even as they betray it. Thus Lovett accepts the 'little object' and a socialist heritage from McLeod:

Thus the actions of people and not their sentiments make history. There was a sentence for it. 'Men enter into social and economic relations independent of their wills,' and did it not mean more than all the drums of the medicine men?[44]

But the quotation from Marx is essentially a departure point for Lovett, from which he proceeds in a totally different direction from that taken by McLeod. To counteract the fact that 'men enter into social and economic relations independent of their wills', the individual must take wilful and direct action against the social determinants of his situation. This, I think, is the philosophical conclusion which emerges at the end of *Barbary Shore* and which is developed more fully in Mailer's next novel, *The Deer Park*. And this and the view of human nature as an 'open question', together with the existentialist emphasis on 'action' and 'will', are perhaps what Mailer meant when he described his second novel as 'the first of the existentialist novels of America'.[45]

The fictional world of Mailer's third novel, published in 1955, again presents mankind drifting downwards into moral darkness. Desert D'Or, a modern counterpart of Deer Park – Louis XV's orgiastic playground – is revealed as a counterfeit paradise concealing a hell on earth.* The desert setting serves

---

* In *Advertisements for Myself* (p. 312), Mailer comments when adapting a novel into a play: 'When I was doing *The Deer Park* as a novel, characters existed on one level. It seemed to me that putting them into Hell deepened the

as a metaphor for the spiritual and sexual wasteland that the resort really is. Coming to it as a newcomer, Sergius understands that Desert D'Or is 'The imaginery world'[46] and not the real world:

> a world of wars and boxing clubs and children's homes on backstreets, and this real world was a world where orphans burned orphans.[47]

The harsh realities of that world go on outside the enclosed park and O'Shaughnessy, Faye, Eitel and Elena are the characters with the 'passion and consciousness' to see through the appearances of Desert D'Or to a reality which distinguishes sex from love, commercialism from creativity and actions from 'sentiment'. For this reason they stand out against the other residents of Desert D'Or and against the vision of Herman Teppis, head of Supreme Pictures, who sees the resort in terms of romance, as

> A musical. It's full of cowboys and these fellows that live alone, what do you call them, hermits.[48]

There are in fact three heroes to the novel: Eitel the 'potential artist' and professional film direcor, Marion Faye the nihilistic pimp and pusher to the film world, and Sergius O'Shaughnessy, the would-be writer and narrator of the novel. Despite the fact that Faye emerges as the novel's ultimate hero, the centre of the story is Eitel and his failure as a creative writer and director and his capitulation to the commercial world. The parallel and counterpart of this defeat is his denial and devaluation of his relationship with Elena. In his depiction of the two-fold and interrelated failure, Mailer realises the intention he referred to in *Advertisements for Myself* of telling:

> the more painful story of two people who are strong as well as weak, corrupt as much as pure, and fail to grow despite their bravery in a poor world, because they are finally not brave enough, and so do more damage to one another than to the unjust world outside them.[49]

It is however more difficult to analyse the role of Faye and

---

meaning of their moral experience. That the situation of being in Hell and not knowing it . . . is the first dislocation of the moral space.'

O'Shaughnessy because of the obvious gap between the author's intention and his achievement.

Sergius O'Shaughnessy is offered as a contrast to Eitel in so far as he resists the temptations of Desert D'Or and is shown ultimately as achieving a measure of integrity as a writer. Although this creativity is formally asserted, he is too inadequately realised as a character to carry the heroic qualities that the end of the novel endows him with. He introduces himself as a conventional war-hero, a pilot who had been decorated for his part in the Asiatic war. In appearance he is a stereotype of the Hollywood male fantasy-hero with 'blond hair and blue eyes . . . and six foot one' with 'the build of a light heavy-weight'.[50] Nevertheless he cannot take his image for the 'real thing' and this fact together with his ability to distinguish between the real world and the imaginery world 'in which almost everybody lived'[51] is the measure of his heroic potential:

> When I would put on my uniform, I would feel like an unemployed actor who tries to interest a casting director by dressing for the role.[52]

But his carefully asserted abilities drop out of sight in the sections dealing with Eitel and Elena, and when the novel returns to him to describe his affair with Lulu there is little evidence of either the passion or consciousness of a hero; nor do his activities in Mexico and New York establish these qualities. Further, in the face of the scrupulously documented forces working against both love and creative work, his semi-mystical vision of hope and renewal at the end of the novel appears weak and unreal:

> Then for a moment in that cold Irish soul of mine, a glimmer of the joy of the flesh came toward me, rare as the eye of the rarest tear of compassion, and we laughed together after all, because to have heard that sex was time and time the connection of new circuits was a part of the poor odd dialogues which give hope to us noble humans for more than one night.[53]

The nihilistic despair of Marion Faye emerges as a much more valid response to these forces than Sergius' glib enigma of Time. Since the novel presents such a strong vision of corruption, confusion and deception, despair seems an appropriate emotional direction for the novel's hero to take. Faye, like O'Shaughnessy, serves as a foil for Eitel but also exists as an independent and positive figure. To both, Eitel initially represents some kind of model or hero, but Faye judges him quickly and ruthlessly when he sees Eitel betraying those principles. His admiration changes to hatred, as he tells Eitel,

> Because you might have been an artist, and you spit on it.[54]

Faye himself is presented as an inverted puritan in search of moral purity, or, as Sergius says to him:

> You're just a religious man turned inside out.[55]

He will not settle for Ridges' and Goldstein's 'goodness' in 'humiliating failure', but finding himself in the vicious corrupt and dishonest world of Desert D'Or, he forces himself to master all its vices, hence his role in the town. His fear of self-deception and compromise with sentimentality leads to his attempt to live entirely without sentiment. This idealist search for emotional purity is his goal in refusing the Mexican addict, Paco's, plea for money for drugs. After Paco departs, Faye theorises:

> Once you knew that guilt was the cement of the world, there was nothing to it; you could own the world, or spit at it. But first you had to get rid of your own guilt, and to do that you had to kill compassion. Compassion was the queen of guilt.[56]

Armed with this 'cool' perception that the vital element in fear is guilt, Faye trains himself to feel none of the guilt which weakens people, hoping in this way to achieve the strength (and nobility) to withstand the values of his time. But his absolutism becomes an end in itself:

> Nobility and vice – they're the same thing. It just depends on the direction you're going. You see, if I ever make it, then I turn around and go the other way. Toward nobility. That's all right. Just so you carry it to the end.[57]

Although Faye does not make it 'to the end' ('he and his drop of mercy after all'[58]), what this position points toward is made clear in his apocalyptic vision of annihilation:

So let it come, Faye thought, let this explosion come, and then another, and all the others, until the Sun God burned the earth. Let it come, he thought, looking into the east at Mecca where the bombs ticked while he stood on a tiny rise of ground . . . Let it come, Faye begged, like a man praying for rain, let it come and clear away the rot and the stench and the stink, let it come for all of everywhere, just so it comes and the world stands clear in the white dead dawn.[59]

Faye's need is, as Mailer comments, for 'a point of the compass, any point, and he could follow it on some black heroic safari'[60], but the point, the quest for the heroic, lapses into a desire for destruction. Mailer plainly endorses his hero's obsession with courage – action rather than sentiment – and holds up for admiration his 'passion and consciousness', but he offsets Faye's despair with his other hero's note of hope – his 'glimmer of joy'.[61]

Nevertheless it is in the pathological Faye that Mailer's more lasting prototypes of a hero take shape. Eitel, the most fully developed of Mailer's tragic liberal heroes whose antecedents are Hearn and McLeod, has no issue in the later novels. However, I think Mailer expresses more of his ideas on the heroic *by negation* (in his depiction of Eitel's failure) than in his attempts to give them positive form with O'Shaughnessy and Faye. In a sense he takes over where Fitzgerald left off in *The Last Tycoon*. Both Monroe Starr and Eitel are caught up in the contradictions of the film industry as business and art. Fitzgerald's hero is conceived in the old romantic-hero mould, as one who can overcome these contradictions by virtue of his personal qualities, whereas Mailer demonstrates the futility of such ideas in his account of Eitel's career with Supreme Pictures. At the start

> he was full of the premise that to make the movies he wanted, he had to be powerful.[62]

His career continues, his salary increases, but he never gains the power to make films which are 'art' rather than good business. He compromises; the actors, story and plot are furnished by Supreme Pictures and he supplies a certain 'atmosphere'.[63] He becomes a professional on an assembly line* which pro-

* 'The qualities of the film industry in Hollywood are the qualities of any big

duces a product in a market situation and consoles himself for
the lack of artistic power with the consumer power that money
gives him:

> a fourteen room house with a library, a wine closet, a gymna-
> sium, a swimming pool.[64]

Having spent nearly twenty years making films for Supreme
Pictures, and losing all autonomy as a creative director, he
attempts to break away from the pattern by refusing to testify to
a Congressional Committee ('the reason I acted that way with
the Committee was to give myself another chance'.)[65] His
struggle to write the script he'd been 'saving for years' recalls
McLeod's decision, after twenty years as a Party bureaucrat, to
return to theory. In this novel the process is followed through –
to failure. Eitel relinquishes the attempt when he accepts
Munshin's distortion of his precious script and he is forced to
recognise how, fundamentally, he shares Munshin's values:

> The professional in Eitel lusted for the new story; it was so
> perfect for a profitable movie, it was so beautifully false. Pro-
> fessional blood thrived on what was excellently dishonest,
> and Collie had given him the taste of that again.[66]

He fails to establish a new identity as an artist because he
cannot transcend his own history as a commercial director. He
is therefore, in terms of the distinctions Mailer developed in his
first two novels, determined by his situation rather than the
hero who transcends that situation:

> Life has made me a determinist, he thought in passing.[67]

The professionalism which undermines his creative abilities
is also present in his sexual relationships. Like other members
of the Desert D'Or film world, he had come to regard sex in
terms of technique and egotism:

> To be a good lover . . . one should be incapable of falling in
> love.[68]

At the start of his affair with Elena Esposito, he is merely elated

---

American industry: machine-tool technology, division of labour, mass production, bureaucracy, hierarchy . . .' (Max Lerner, *America as a Civilisation*,
pp. 823–4. Quoted by Millgate in *American Social Fiction*.)

by their performance, but as he becomes more involved, he recognises that she represents 'a chance' for him to go beyond his
usual experiences:

> With this girl it was impossible to thrive in the world except
> by his art, and for these weeks, these domestic weeks when all
> went well and the act of sitting beside her in the sun could
> give him a sense of strength and the confidence of liking him-
> self, he would feel indifference to that world which he had
> found it so hard to leave.[69]

In this passage, with great economy, Mailer reveals the axis on
which their relationship turns and at the same time establishes
the core of his theme – the interrelationship between integrity
and work and the ability to love. 'When all went well' brings out
an implied threat to their relationship; if Eitel cannot thrive by
his art, he cannot sustain any feelings for Elena.

His work on the script goes badly and the reasons for this are
clearly presented. In this he resembles the writer in Baldwin's
Another Country who tells himself that he writes pot-boilers to
earn the time and money to write 'seriously' and then discovers
he can only operate on this level. Silenski expresses his guilt and
disappointment in aggression towards his wife and Eitel reacts
in a similar way after he stops believing in his script:

> Under such a burden, he was growing critical of Elena's
> faults. He would wince as he watched her eat, for she waved
> her fork, her mouth often full as she spoke.[70]

The simplicity which he at first admired, he begins to see as ignorance and awkwardness and he is ashamed of her in the company of those he himself despises. When he decides to sell the
rights of the script (the 'professional' one) to Munshin, he realises that he dreads telling Elena. She, along with Faye, recognises the significance of his decision to give up 'till later' any
real attempt to write. As he establishes a friendly working relationship with Munshin, the tension between Eitel and Elena
increases; he grows to dislike her and decides to end their relationship. Finding 'love' too difficult to sustain, he returns to
'sentiment' which is signalled in the episode with the call-girl
Bobby. His sentimentality here is described so as to resemble

the imprecise, self-indulgent feelings aroused by a Supreme
Pictures movie, for,

> Like most cynics he was profoundly sentimental about sex.[71]

As he resumes the role of professional in his work so he
resumes the role of a professional lover, experienced in having
'affairs' and skilled in ending them. Mailer charts this process
in Eitel in detail:

> For the first time since he had been living with Elena, he
> found himself repeating the emotions of many old affairs.
> The time had come to decide how he would break up with
> her. This was always delicate . . . .[72]

Just as his professionalism (technique) in his work allows him
to be detached from the content of the film (now entitled 'Saints
and Lovers'), so he uses his expertise as a lover to distance himself from the meaning of the breakup—the problem becomes *how*
to end the affair and not *why*. His refusal to risk himself in the relationship and in his work constitutes a betrayal of his own definition of heroism:

> The essence of spirit, he thought to himself, was to choose the
> thing which did not better one's position but made it more
> perilous.[73]

The index of his deterioration is contained in the passages
where Eitel *does* attempt to analyse his relationship, his reflections exemplify that blend of reality and dishonesty which he
describes in successful movie-making. He dislikes her, he
admits to himself, 'for her sullenness, her vulgarity, her love
itself'.[74] This is of course true and yet 'beautifully false': what
he dislikes her for is her insight into what he is doing and her
failure to sympathise with it. Rueful when other men like
O'Shaughnessy and Faye judge him, he finds it intolerable that
Elena, 'his woman', should do the same. Although she cannot
articulate them, she holds the 'serious' values he professes, or
professed, to hold. He does indeed dislike her awkwardness for
it is a symptom of her anti-professionalism, the fact that she is
'an amateur in Love'[75] as he realised earlier on.

   Thus in his sustained study of Eitel and Elena's relationship,
Mailer not only shows Eitel's failure to rise to heroic stature, he

develops the antitheses which are the offshoots of his original polarity between 'the beast and the seer in man': creativity and professionalism, sentimentality and love, and consciousness and determinism.

A COLLECTION OF POSSIBILITIES

Although Mailer did not create another fictional hero for some nine years (until the publication of *An American Dream* in 1964), his interim work collected in *Advertisements for Myself* (1959) and *The Presidential Papers* (1963) is explicitly concerned with the need for a hero and crystallises many of the ideas present in *The Deer Park*. In that novel, it is noticeable that animal imagery, in so far as it is used at all, is used to convey a new and more positive meaning than it had in *The Naked and the Dead* and *Barbary Shore*. It is Elena who is described as 'as wild and sensitive as an animal'[76] and of whom the sophisticated (and deteriorating) Eitel says it was 'as if he'd asked a subtle animal to share his house'.[77] Besides subtlety and sensitivity, O'Shaughnessy connects animal qualities with the energy and courage he had discovered in boxing:

> It seems to come from way inside, like you're a dying animal, maybe.[78]

The 'beast,' it seems, can have heroic possibilities as well as the 'seer'.

In *Advertisements for Myself* the instinctual life with which these images are associated is the means by which Mailer's various heroes (and that includes Mailer himself) survive and challenge the 'totalitarian tissues of American society'[79]; the 'cool' hipster living on his instincts and nerves is opposed to the sentimental conformist Square. The emphasis has shifted from McLeod's prescription for 'men of . . . *consciousness* and passion' to a new prescription for courage and the 'secrets of that inner *unconscious* life which will nourish you'.[80] The shift is predictable given Mailer's view of American society: in a totalitarian State which invades every aspect of one's conscious life, the possibilities for a dynamic, heroic consciousness are limited, therefore Mailer transfers his hopes to the unconscious – the psychic levels. The hero of the story 'The Man Who Studied Yoga', himself a novelist, comments on the difficulties of creating fictional heroes:

> One could not have a hero today, Sam thinks, a man of action
> and contemplation capable of sin, large enough for good, a
> man immense. There is only a modern hero damned by no
> more than the ugliness of wishes whose satisfaction he will
> never know. One needs a man who could walk the stage,
> someone who – no matter who, not himself. Someone, Sam
> thinks, who reasonably could not exist.[81]

In 'The White Negro' Mailer does create just such a hero – a
hipster – 'who reasonably could not exist'. It becomes apparent
that the essay is not principally concerned with the Negro,
white or black, hipster or square, but with a celebration of 'instinct' or one of its synonyms. Instinct, the defining quality of
Mailer's 'White Negro', becomes the hero of the essay. Mailer's
interest in the American hipster stems from the fact that he sees
them (or imagines them) as living out their instincts, particularly their sexual instincts:

> But to be with it is to have grace, is to be closer to the secrets
> of that inner unconscious life which will nourish you if you
> can hear it, for you are then nearer to that God which every
> hipster believes is located in the senses of his body, that
> trapped, mutilated and nonetheless megalomaniacal God
> who is It, who is energy, life, sex, force, the Yoga's *prana*, the
> Reichian's orgone, Lawrence's 'blood,' Hemingway's
> 'Good,' the Shavian life-force; 'It'; God; not the God of the
> churches but the unachievable whisper of mystery within the
> sex, the paradise of limitless energy and perception just
> beyond the next wave of the next orgasm.[82]

A close discussion of these ideas and attitudes belongs to the
chapter on Mailer's approach to sexuality and women, but an
outline of his 'mysticism of the flesh' is important for an understanding of his later heroes – Rojack and DJ in particular.

Entwined with the nostalgia for the primitive, instinctual life
and the search for the apocalyptic orgasm in 'The White
Negro' is his concern with the possibilities of freedom and
choice. The ideas put forward are basically those of McLeod
that 'human potential is an open question' reinforced however

by the language of existentialism:

> each man is glimpsed as a collection of possibilities, some
> more possible than others (the view of character implicit in
> Hip) and some humans are considered more capable than
> others of reaching more possibilities within themselves in less
> time.[83]

In 'Hip, Hell and the Navigator' and in the 'Hipsters' section of
Advertisements for Myself he develops this view, not in existential
language but using the theological (or eschatalogical) metaphors of God and the Devil which are found in his work from
this time onwards. Man's fate, he suggests, is bound up with
God's fate and God is no longer all-powerful:

> He is not all-powerful. He exists as a warring element in a
> divided universe, and we are a part of – perhaps the most
> important part of – His great expression, His enormous des-
> tiny; perhaps He is trying to impose upon the universe His
> conception of being against other conceptions of being very
> much opposed to His. Maybe we are in a sense the seed, the
> seed-carriers, the voyagers, the explorers, the embodiment of
> that embattled vision; maybe we are engaged in a heroic ac-
> tivity, and not a mean one.[84]

This concept of man as the emissaries in God's 'embattled
vision' started, I believe, as a metaphor to convey Mailer's ideas
on free will and determinism, but became much more than
metaphorical. It offered him an explanation of evil, 'thrilling
new moral complexities'[85] and a new formulation of man's
heroic role. How this new antithesis of God and the Devil is
superimposed on Mailer's previously developed oppositions
becomes obvious in *The Presidential Papers*. God is associated
with inspiration and instincts and the Devil with all that is 'professional':

> If God and the Devil are locked in an implacable war, it
> might not be excessive to assume their powers are separate,
> God the lord of inspiration, the Devil a monumental bureau-
> crat of repetition. To learn from an inner voice the first time it
> speaks to us is a small bold existential act, for it depends
> upon following one's instinct which must derive, in no matter
> how distorted a fashion, from God, whereas institutional

knowledge is appropriated by the Devil.[86]

In *The Presidential Papers* (1963) Mailer discusses his search for a hero in two essays, 'Heroes and Leaders' and 'The Existential Hero'. His 'seed-carriers, voyagers and explorers' are no longer looked for in the ranks of the pathological; his hopes of the hipster as a satanic hero have faded in a culture where hipsters now abound – 'a horde of half-begotten Christs with straggly beards, heroes none, saints all . . .'[87] In desperation at the powerlessness of these psychic outlaws, Mailer searches for a hero among public figures: writers like Hemingway, boxers like Patterson, and the then President John F. Kennedy.

Kennedy has the traits of a 'Sergius O'Shaughnessy born rich'[88] and Mailer outlines his possibilities as a hero with the now familiar emphasis on courage – physical and mental:

> a war hero, and the heroism is bona-fide, even exceptional, a man who has lived with death, who crippled in the back took on an operation which would kill him or restore him to power.[89]

Kennedy's somewhat basic qualifications are given a philosophical dimension by Mailer's argument that

> Existential politics is rooted in the concept of the hero, it would argue that the hero is the one kind of man who never develops by accident, that a hero is a consecutive set of brave and witty self-creations.[90]

'Never' accents Mailer's disbelief in chance or determinism and his commitment to existential freedom. The need for a national hero stems from the idea that state authority should be individualised – 'Power without a face is the disease of the state.'[91] The life of politics and the life of myth have diverged too far and the old legends and American myths which held 'that each man was born to be free, to wander, to have adventure and to grow'[92] have been exhausted. The need is now for an individual hero, not with consciousness but with the ability to plumb the repressed desires and myths of America's unconscious:

> It was a hero America needed, a hero central to his time, a man whose personality might suggest contradictions and mysteries which would reach into the alienated circuits of the

underground, because only a hero can capture the secret imagination of a people, and so be good for the vitality of his nation; a hero embodies the fantasy and so allows each private mind the liberty to consider its fantasy and find a way to grow.[93]

This statement points straight to Mailer's next fictional hero – Rojack, but it is difficult even in his own terms to adapt it to Kennedy. The essay as a whole moves uneasily between Kennedy the Presidential candidate and then President, and Mailer's development of his ideal existential hero. Mailer acknowledges something of this in his criticisms of Kennedy's 'dullness', his lack of imagination.

The professional–amateur metaphors express this confusion. The definition of the professional in 'Heroes and Leaders' is of one who can manipulate the best single elements in the old solutions but who can never create a new solution because 'what they lack in imagination is filled with strategic estimate'.[94] Thus the professionals who advise the President are 'dishonest because they are professional'[95], and on the logic of this argument Mailer compiled his Presidential Papers. The President's advisors are incapable of doing more than tinker with machinery of government because they are encapsulated within it. It takes an amateur (like Mailer) who is outside the structure to describe it accurately, to see new solutions, in short, to give 'honest' advice. But the amateur–professional distinction proves an inadequate basis on which to write about a modern state and the functions of its president. As an approach it is, like the role of 'court wit' which Mailer assumes for himself, anachronistic, but it is also naive in 'a peculiarly American' sense.* Even within the terms of Mailer's metaphor, the President is a professional politician (necessarily) and like all professionals 'dishonest' and therefore ineligible for the heroic role.

But if the essay bills Kennedy as a 'hero' in a romantic and not an existential way, it also undercuts its own claims in a fairly consistent manner. In the section describing the Democratic convention Mailer focuses attention on Kennedy's image

* *The Naked and the Dead*, p. 320. Mailer's political hopes here resemble those of one of his earliest 'heroes', General Cummings whose romantic zeal in political negotiations is called 'peculiarly American' by his European counterparts.

and personality on the justification that his political programme is well-documented elsewhere. The imagery used is a
comment on the unreality of American party politics, but one
that includes Kennedy in its irony:

> he made his way inside surrounded by a mob, and one
> expected at any moment to see him lifted to its shoulders like
> a matador being carried back to the city after a triumph in
> the plaza. All'the while the band kept playing the campaign
> tunes, sashaying circus music, and one had a moment of clar-
> ity, intense as a *deja vu*, for the scene which had taken place
> had been glimpsed before in a dozen musical comedies; it
> was a scene where the hero, the matinee idol, the movie star
> comes to the palace to claim the princess . . .[96]

The point that Convention politics are mainly pageantry –
mass entertainment – is kept alive in the frequent references to
American film actors; Kennedy is most often compared with
Brando, whereas Johnson is a Broderick Crawford or a Paul
Douglas villain. With his 'ski-instructor's suntan' and his
'amazingly white teeth'[97] Kennedy emerges from this treatment as in fact a mass-entertainment hero; the words 'king' and
'prince' begin to replace the term 'hero' and the existential
claims made on his behalf fade from view. Near the end of the
essay, the fictional nature of Kennedy's charisma is acknowledged in a pointed comparison with the rich, young heroes of
Scott Fitzgerald:

> The legend of Fitzgerald had an army at last, formed around
> the self-image in the mind of every superior Madison Avenue
> opportunist that he was hard, he was young, he was In, his
> conversation was lean as wit, and if the work was not always
> scrupulous, well the style could aspire.[98]

The conclusion is fairly clear; having articulated his demands,
Mailer tried to supply them, tried to invest Kennedy with the
properties and potential of the 'hero America needed', and he
failed.*

---

* Despite this, in the preface to the Presidential Papers written after
Kennedy's assassination, Mailer maintains the existential possibilities of
Kennedy having *become* heroic: 'he wasn't a great man . . . He was a man who
could have become great or could have failed, and now we'll never know.
(p.8)

The hero of the novel he wrote a year later, *An American Dream* (1964), is a man who unlike Kennedy failed to become President, and the reasons for this failure are this time presented as a central part of his heroism. He introduces himself as a former friend of Kennedy's and a fellow war-hero but from there the emphasis is on their differences. Still obsessed by Kennedy's crucial flaw, lack of imagination, Mailer creates a hero with a superhuman imagination whose whole dream is, in one sense, an excercise of the artistic imagination. And this time he places his Kierkegaardian hero outside of politics. This shift, which reflects, I think, his disillusionment with political leaders as heroes, together with his concentration on the dream-life of the nation, was foreshadowed in the essay 'On Dread':

> But then politics, like journalism, is interested to hide from us the existential abyss of dread, the terror which lies beneath our sedation. Today, a successful politician is not a man who wrestles with the art of the possible . . . he is, on the contrary, a doctor of mass communications who may measure his success by the practice of a political ritual and vocabulary which diverts us temporarily from dread, from anxiety, from the mirror of the dream.[99]

The ordeal of Stephen Rojack is precisely what Mailer terms an 'anxiety dream' which constantly examines 'how much anxiety can you take'. (Mailer in the Skelling interview cited in Kaufman.) The American dream has turned into a nightmare of material success, but Rojack's dream of ecstasy and violence underlies the 'sedation' of American life and therefore is authentic and potentially liberating for the American nation. Before his dream begins he has exhausted all the possibilities of growth provided by his culture; his forty-four years include a Phi Beta Kappa, *summa cum laude*, the Distinguished Service Cross, Congress, academic acclaim, television exposure, a beautiful heiress as wife and all the conventional successes of the American Dream. Nevertheless, he, like O'Shaughnessy, rejects this past as inauthentic – 'I remained an actor. My personality was built upon a void'[100] – and he has come to decide that he is 'finally a failure'.[101] His rejection of politics and other forms of the American Dream of power is based on his wartime experiences of a different kind of power. Nothing in his rational view of the world explains this experience of the 'existential abyss of dread', but it was a sufficiently 'religious' event to set him apart from the conventional heroes of his culture:

> The real difference between the President and myself may be that I ended with too large an appreciation of the moon, for I looked down the abyss on the first night I killed: four men, four very separate Germans, dead under a full moon – whereas Jack, for all I know, never saw the abyss.[102]

The relevance of Rojack's dream to America's need for a hero is established not only in the title of the novel but also in the references to Kennedy, Hemingway, Marilyn Monroe and other current American culture-symbols. His adventures in the thirty-two hours of the novel are not just an 'assortment of dull cruelties and callous copulations', as Elizabeth Hardwick's review called them, but the spiritual travails of one of the 'voyagers and explorers' in God's 'embattled vision'. To liberate himself from the violence and perversions of what Mailer sees as the American way of life, Rojack decides that he must, like Marion Faye, 'make it to the end' – act out the dream fantasies of his culture in order to reach a new state of consciousness. His pilgrimage through this psychic terrain towards the 'heavenly city'[103] is consistently described in religious imagery.

The poles of good and evil, God and the Devil are interlinked with a series of oppositions: the rational and the instinctive, the intellectual and the mystical, the conscious and the unconscious. At the start of the story the narrator-hero introduces himself as a man seeking alternatives to intellectuality and rational explanations of experience:

> There are times when I like to think I still have my card in the intellectual's guild, but I seem to be joining company with that horde of the mediocre and the mad who listen to popular songs and act upon coincidence.[104]

The intellectuals are the minority, the élite, who attempt to live rationally and who dismiss instinctive behaviour along with mass entertainment. Rojack is a possible hero of his time because he straddles the world of the 'horde' and that of the

'guild'; he sees himself as a renegade intellectual turned theo-
retician for the non-intellectual majority. This unifying role is
indicated by his position in the intellectual-rational world of
the University, which is to propound the irrational, mystical
elements in human behaviour:

> I was now at a university in New York, a professor of existen-
> tial psychology with the not inconsiderable thesis that magic,
> dread, and the perception of death were the roots of motiva
> tion.[105]

In effect, he takes this thesis out of the classroom and into his
(dream) life. At the party before he visits his wife, he experiences an extreme state of 'nausea' in both the physical and the
Sartrean sense. Resisting his instinct to commit suicide, he feels
impelled to see Deborah, his estranged wife, whom he had married nine years previously at the height of his ambitions towards
the Presidency. Their marriage had been many things to him,
his 'entry to the big league', the 'armature of my ego',[106] 'a
devil's contract'.[107] She is thus a symbol of his inauthentic past
and an expression of all the destructive and negative aspects of
his present existence. Their marriage had been a war which
had never been resolved, and whose continuance saps the
hero's strength and morale. Rojack murders her therefore, because at the allegorical level of the novel, she represents the
forces of darkness from which he must free himself, before he
can live in the present. She is the beast whom the intending
'seer' must conquer or destroy. Further, from her death he
hopes to inherit her powers and her 'light' which she cannot
take to the underworld:

> She was bad in death. A beast stared back at me. Her teeth
> showed, the point of light in her eye was violent, and her
> mouth was open. It looked like a cave. I could hear some
> wind which reached down to the cellars of a sunless earth. A
> little line of spit came from the corner of her mouth, and at an
> angle from her nose one green seed had floated its small dis-
> tance on an abortive rill of blood.[108]

By murdering his evil spirit, Rojack gains a new life and a 'new
grace';[109] he has saved himself from the plight of the autopsy-
subject whose cancer, Mailer suggests, is the result of denying

his murderous impulses:

> and *crack* the door flew open and the wire tore in her throat, and I was through the door, hatred passing from me in wave after wave, illness as well, rot and pestilence, nausea, a bleak string of salts. I was floating. I was as far into myself as I had ever been and universes wheeled in a dream.[110]

The opening of the 'door' – doors, gates and portals are used as images for the barriers between the subconscious and consciousness – gives him his first glimpse of the 'heavenly city', but the battle is only beginning.

> I had had a view of what was on the other side of the door, and heaven was there . . .[111]

He then encounters the temptations and possibilities represented by Ruta and Cherry, and moves inexorably toward a confrontation with the Devil, equipped only with his courage and with Shago's umbrella as his sword. Shago is of course a rival not merely for Cherry but for the heroic role, but is disqualified by his loss of courage and therefore beaten up by Rojack and kicked 'downstairs'. Entering the Waldorf to encounter Kelly, Rojack is struck with fear and trembling and the significance of the moment to the allegory is made explicit:

> for a moment I had died and was in the antechamber of Hell. I had a long vision of Hell: not of its details; of its first moment.[112]

His 'sword' registers the vibrations of evil but his courage is not only his chief weapon but his standard 'for I believed that God was not love but courage.[113] The anguish he suffers is sacrificial in that he goes to purge not only his individual guilt and fear but also that of America. Rojack's temptation at Kelly's hands is intended as America's since he, a 'minor saint', does battle with Kelly, a 'little devil', who has given his allegiance to the powers of darkness in America. The issue is whether devils or saints will determine America's moral character. Heroically, our hero risks his life and sanity in this cause, for his journey into himself entails a struggle with dread and the abyss; his mental life is split into a 'voice' and a 'mind' with messages coming from both God and the Devil. He must battle with the Devil whilst balancing on the brink (the parapet) of schizophrenia, liable to plunge at any moment into the abyss of madness, for,

> There was nothing so delicate in all the world as one's last touch of control.[114]

At the end of the novel, Mailer leaves his hero's position in doubt. In the desert outside Las Vegas Rojack claims to be part of 'a new breed of man',[115] having triumphed over cancer, suicide and madness; but his vision of the Celestial City is qualified by the ambiguous* nature of that heaven and by his final helplessness before it:

> There was a jewelled city on the horizon, spires rising in the night, but the jewels were diadems of electric and the spires were the neon of signs ten stories high. I was not good enough to climb up and pull them down.[116]

His flight from Las Vegas to central America suggests that his dream has gone beyond the limits of American experience, and Rojack ends as a sub-culture hero with no workable roots in national reality. If Faye sought to escape the 'rot and the stench' in his vision of total annihilation, Rojack escapes the 'rot and the perstilence'[117] in his dream of individual murder; Mailer in his final (and most desperate) version of this kind of hero, has DJ 'escape the mixed shit' of 'syphilisation' only to discover that

> God was a beast, not a man, and God said, 'Go out and kill – fulfill my will, go and kill.'[118]

DJ, the 'shit-oriented late adolescent'[119] hero of *Why are We in Vietnam?* (1967), has the qualities of Mailer's other existential heroes. *He* is 'up tight with the concept of dread',[120] teeters on the brink of the abyss ('Grand Synthesizer of the Modern Void'[121]), goes through his own 'purification ceremony'[122] as a trial of his courage and ability to live with both anxiety and the fact of death, and last but not least (the indelible mark of

---

* 'Then I saw that there was a way to hell, even from the gates of heaven, as well as from the City of Destruction. So I awoke and behold it was a dream.' Christian's last words at the end of Part 1 of *The Pilgrim's Progress*. Mailer's use of Bunyan and the allegorical tradition is referred to in Chapter 3 of this study.

Mailer's existential heroes) is endowed with an acute sense of smell. As a hero though he differs in two key respects: he is presented as a comic-hero in ways which Faye and Rojack clearly are not, and, since in this novel character gives way to language, he exists as the 'voice' of the novel rather than just its 'hero'.

In Mailer's early and middle work the conflict between the beast and the seer verges on fatal resolution (those times when the beast in man seems powerful enough to become his own 'seer') but is narrowly averted. In *Why are We in Vietnam?* Mailer attempts to resolve the conflict by objectifying the murderous impulse in man – deciding in fact, that it stems from God. The man-beast dichotomy, expressed formally in the narrative occasion, is the shaping vision of the novel. The theme is maintained from the references to 'animal murder of the soldierest sort' on the first page to the revelation given to DJ and Tex at the close of the novel that 'God was a beast and not a man'.[123] This metaphysical theme is interwoven with the theme of the social conflict between civilisation (man) and the natural (animal) world and with the political symbolism based on specific animals (e.g. the Eagle and America) together with much incidental animal imagery.

The narrative occasion is in fact a hunting expedition in Alaska undertaken by a group of Texans. Apart from the titular reference Vietnam is mentioned only on the last page, but Mailer having posed the question 'Why are we in Vietnam?' attempts to answer it by making the hunt a symbol for war and by constructing an allegorical exposition of the American psyche. The hunt which takes Rusty, DJ, Tex and the others to the frontiers of civilisation can be seen broadly in that tradition of American literature which deals with the relation of man to nature; specifically the book is full of echoes of Hemingway and Faulkner. The members of the expedition are from the 'Electrox Edison world, all programmed out',[124] from the heart of Corporation land – in Mailer's terms the non-vital, plague-infested, technology-bound America – and they travel to the 'land of the icy wilderness and the lost peaks and the unseen deep and the spires, crystal receiver of the continent'.[125] In its narrative situation then, the novel stands in ironic relation to the tradition of the pastoral which runs through American writing; that tradition which presents 'nature' – a landscape either wild or, if cultivated, rural – as a repository of values, order and happiness. It stands, in twentieth century America, in contrast to an industrial, urbanised and intricately organised modern society. The lyricism of the passages describing the forests and snow-fields of the Arctic circle in *Why are We in Vietnam?* does suggest, unironically, a garden with prelapserian qualities.

One of the most insistently made points in the treatment of the civilisation and nature theme is, of course, that the hunters take their 'Electrox Edison' world with them. Brooks Range is a parody of the wild frontier situation in that it is an exclusive playground for American politicians and business executives who frequent it for status or escapist reasons. There are no Major de Spains or Compsons in the Moe Henry clientele. The bear in *Why are We in Vietnam?*, although it symbolises the force and mystery of the animal world as it did in Faulkner's story 'The Bear', is a symbol in a different and debased world, as the language of the hunters suggests – ('Grizzer', 'Baron Bear' and 'Grizz 1 and 2').

There is an obvious parallel between Tex and DJ's renunciation of their weapons and equipment in order to open themselves to the authentic experience of the wilderness, and the renunciation of watch and compass as 'tainted' by Isaac McCaslin in 'The Bear' (*Go Down Moses*)[126]. There is also a contrasting parallel between Luke Fellinka and Faulkner's creation of Sam Fathers. Big Luke is a modern corrupt version of Fathers as the professional hunter, the acknowledged priest of the hunting ceremony. There is also the implied relationship between Mailer's guide and Hemingway's hunter-cognescenti-real man figure ('Big Luke got a presence'[127]). In Hemingway no serious conflict is permitted between the hunter-guide's professionalism and the integrity whim Hemingway usually bestows on such characters. In *Why are We in Vietnam?* Luke's professionalism is one of the reasons for his corruption:

Big Luke used to be a big hunter, but those grizzly scratches have weakened his Arnold Toynbee co-efficient – he is interested less in challenge than in response – if he caught his share of the three grand a head . . . well, Big Luke despite the big man death-guts charisma, may have had his day. Who's to say there is no actors in Alaska?[128]

Significantly, when Tex and DJ break away from the Cop-Turd expedition to take their 'purification ceremony'[129] they leave Big Luke with Rusty and the Medium Assholes. The modern hero has to define himself *against* his culture. The last statement in the passage quoted above implies that not only Big Luke the individual 'may have had his day' but that in contemporary America, the whole type is obsolete – they only mimic the heroic posture of Faulkner's and Hemingway's hunters.

Liberated from paternal authority by Rusty's cowardice, DJ shifts his instincts for love and battle to his symbolic brother, his other self who faces with him the anxieties of travelling without gun or knife and the 'Awe-Dread Bombardment from Mr Sender'.[130] Through their mutual awareness of their mutual desire for sex and fratricide, DJ and Tex finally achieve a sense of purification and solidarity:

> Now it was there, murder between them under all friendship, for God was a beast and not a man, and God said, 'Go out and kill – fulfill my will, go and kill,' and they hung there each of them on the knife of the divide in all conflict of lust to own the other yet in fear of being killed by the other and as the hour went by and the lights shifted, something in the radiance of the North went into them, and owned their fear, some communion of telapathies and new powers, and they were twins, never to be as near as lovers again, but killer brothers, owned by something, prince of darkness, lord of light, they did not know; . . . and each bit a drop of blood from his own finger and touched them across and met, blood to blood . . .[131]

DJ's 'heroic' adventure ends on this note of mystical brotherhood, which despite the differences in tone, recalls the image of Goldstein and Ridges sharing the waterbottle on Anopopei beach. The 'brothers' ' awe in the face of natural world is also reminiscent of Goldstein's and Ridges'. DJ's task, as hero of the story, is essentially more modest than that of Rojack and although Mailer makes the same points about America and with the same urgency, there is a new distance and humour apparent in his treatment of his hero:

America, this is your own wandering troubadour brought

right up to date, here to sell America its new handbook on how to live . . .[132]

The seminal concept of dread is translated into the language of rock-and-roll. A vast chasm of culture and sensibility separates the tone of Rojack's agonised monologue from the narrative voice of *Why are We in Vietnam?*

> The world is going shazam, hahray, harout, fart in my toot, air we breathe is the prez, present dent, and God has always wanted more from man than man has wished to give him. Zig a zig a zig. That is why we live in dread of God.[133]

This is partly because the writing itself is intended to be restorative, a blow against the 'totalitarian prose' of the 'communications engineers'.[134] And this attempt to make the language of his fiction itself 'Heroic'[135] suggests a movement away from the 'existential hero' who has dominated Mailer's fiction since *The Deer Park*.

The irony apparent in the treatment of DJ is even more explicit in his latest work, where Mailer makes himself his own hero – thus creating a third heroic type. In *The Armies of the Night* (1968) he created a fictional Norman Mailer in an attempt to produce a voice which comprehends the first-person voice of his essays, but gives that 'I' a fictional existence – a dimension beyond the autobiographical. The Reporter in *Miami and the Siege of Chicago*, Aquarius in *A Fire on the Moon* and the Prisoner in *A Prisoner of Sex* are all creations in the same mode. Whatever this development signifies – whether one sees it as experiment with the fictional forms or as a move from the novel into essay-journalism – the heroes of these last four books are, clearly, closely related to the 'existential hero' typified by Faye, Rojack and DJ. The ways in which they are different are best considered, I think, in the context of a discussion of Mailer's problems with 'voice'. But certainly there is no sign of a return to the earlier heroic model – the Hearn–McLeod-Eitel group of doomed, liberal heroes; these characters, presented as men of considerable intelligence who are 'flawed' by their professionalism or their lack of 'courage', and defeated by the world in which they live, are finally too close to the heroic-type Mailer disliked so intensely in the novels of his contemporaries:

Where the original heroes of naturalism had been active, bold, self-centred, close to tragic, and up to their nostrils in their exertions to advance their own life and force the webs of society, so the hero of moral earnestness, the hero Herzog, and the hero Levin in Malamud's *A New Life*, are men who represent the contrary – passive, timid, other-directed, pathetic, up to the nostrils in anguish: the world is stronger than they are; suicide calls.[136]

In this comment Mailer explains his rejection of the one type of hero for the other in his work: active rather than passive, 'self-centred' rather than 'other-directed', given to murder rather than suicide. The comment and the essay from which it is taken also suggests an explanation for the philosophical development from the somewhat determinist view of human nature in *The Naked and the Dead* to the later existentialist conception of man; his heroes reaffirm a philosophical tradition concerned with anxiety and death in an intellectual climate where Mailer fears concern with the individual is beginning to be replaced by a scientistic, rationalistic mode of thinking. Rather than accept or 'suffer' this at the individual level (which is precisely, in one sense, what Herzog does), Mailer's existential heroes were created to embody their author's 'heroic' challenge to the post-war 'technologising' of America.

2 'A Revolution in the Consciousness of Our Time'

Mailer has consistently defined himself as a radical of one sort or another, and I think that this view of himself, and of his work, is essentially correct. At first sight, only his first two novels are political as such; in his third the focus on social relationships and revolution seems to give way to cultural and philosophical problems – the individual dilemmas of a tragic 'bourgeois' hero and his first 'existentialist' hero. But despite the Marxist emphasis on history and social relationships and the Trotskyist treatment of the Russian Revolution, both *The Naked and the Dead* and *Barbary Shore* contain in embryo the political ideas which he later developed into his criticisms of totalitarianism and mass culture on the one hand, and his hopes for changes in consciousness, a psychic revolution on the other. This chapter is an attempt to give a critical description of the political and ideological movement in his writing and to establish that although there is 'an ideological break' between *The Naked and the Dead* and *Barbary Shore* and his later work, there is also a continuity in the pattern of his political thinking.

In *The Armies of the Night* (1968) Mailer says of himself that 'he had begun as a young ideologue – his mind had been militant with positions fixed in concrete'.[1] The ideological issues of *The Naked and the Dead* are already visible in 'A Calculus at Heaven', the war story written in 1943 before being called up; his political intentions, in other words, pre-dated any experience of the war. Similarly, the decision to place his story in the Pacific rather than Europe was dictated partly by literary considerations (the difficulty of representing European culture in American war-novels) but also, as he tells us in *Advertisements for Myself*, by political reasons:

the Pacific war had a reactionary overtone which my young
progressive-liberal nose smelled with the aid of PM edi-
torials . . .[2]

One of the chief ironies underlying the conflict between the
'fascist' Cummings and the 'progressive-liberal' Hearn is that
they are both officers involved in fighting a war against fascism
with a military instrument which is itself fascistic in organisation, structure and ideology. The American army, as it is por-
trayed in *The Naked and the Dead*, is a hierarchy based on
privilege and power; when Hearn protests that the enlisted men
had not received their share of meat while the officers had
received more than their share, Cummings justifies the situation and explains his view of an army

> to make an army work you have to have every man in it fitted
> into a fear-ladder . . . The army functions best when you're
> frightened of the man above you, and contemptuous of your
> subordinates.[3]

The anti-democratic nature of the army in action is exposed by
cutting between the confused, fragmented experience of the
enlisted men and the highly-structured overall conception of
Cummings. With this device Mailer suggests one of the consequences of the fear-ladder: the enlisted men are reduced in
moral and human terms to a mere physical (animal) participation in the war without any larger comprehension of what is
at stake. One of the main divisions in Second World War novelists is between those who accept this expedient fascism (e.g.
Wouk in *The Caine Mutiny* and at a subtler level, Couzzens in
Guard of Honour) and those who challenge or reject it (Shaw in
The Young Lions, Killens in *And Then We Heard the Thunder* and
Mailer in *The Naked and the Dead*). But *The Naked and the Dead*
offers not merely a political criticism of the army, it gives the
enlisted soldiers a political history of their own. It explains
their actions and attitudes in the army as the products of social
determinants at home – suggesting that (the) war only concentrates and reveals the forces of collective life as they already
exist in the given social organisation.

He does this through the 'Time Machine' device which
enables him to flash back to the civilian life of the platoon

members and the result is a systematic indictment of the racialism, sexual neurosis and economic insecurity in American society. The racialism operating in the platoon is shown to be the product of a white Anglo-Saxon Protestant culture where all minority groups suffer a special psychological burden of being outsiders, while those who share only marginally in the dominant culture compensate in the hatred and oppression of minority groups. The first point is made through the alienation of the Mexican, Martinez, from the others and in the case of Goldstein who is strong, efficient, naturally optimistic and gregarious but who becomes demoralised by the antisemitism, active and passive, of the others. Gallagher, Brown and Wilson illustrate in differing degrees the point about 'compensatory' racialism. Another source of anxiety affecting the soldiers is the all-male virility cult. Those who are successful within this cult – the 'fugging machines' – are marked by their competitiveness and brutality not only towards women but towards the 'feminine' characteristics in other men. For those who 'fail' in the sexual aspects of their lives and marriages, their sense of failure eats away at their confidence, their 'manhood', and has a debilitating destructive effect on their relations with other men.

As success in sex is an ideal in the American ideology, so success in one's economic life is presented as an ideal which most men can never achieve. The struggle in the economic rat-race is shown in all its physical and psychological effects; most of the men in the platoon have internalised the ideology of material success and take their economic failure as a reflection on their merit, their ability, their very identity. Red Valsen is the only drop-out but the nature and consequences of his rebellion are shown within the same economic reality. Polack attempts to escape economic 'failure', that is, his class position in American capitalism, by resorting to illegitimate channels (pimping and the Mafia) and Mailer shows how his attempt to beat the system by becoming an exploiter rather than another exploited victim of the system, corrupts his sexual and social relationships.

With the portrait of Roy Gallagher, Mailer draws together the cultural, sexual and economic threads which, he suggests, make up social life and determine character. The characterisation although schematic, shows Mailer's understanding

of the complexity of the circumstances shaping man's character. Raised in a Studs Lonigan environment in Boston,
Gallagher's personal qualities – his intolerance, ignorance and
viciousness – are situated in the context of his family history,
poverty, lack of education and limited prospects of employment. After a romanticised courtship with a young Irish girl, he
drifts into a marriage which shows every sign of repeating the
worst aspects of his parents' marriage, and which binds him
even more closely to the necessity for working in a series of ill-
paid, menial jobs. At this point he joins Christians United, a
radically reactionary, semi-military organisation whose members are bound together by a common hatred of Jews and Com-
munists. He sells a hate magazine on street corners; he
electioneers against liberal and labour-supported candidates
for office; he drills with old Springfield rifles at secret meetings
once a week. His reasons, it is shown, are only marginally political. Christians United supplies him with a scapegoat for his
frustrations and a possibility (or fantasy) of 'getting ahead' – it
is the lumpen proletariat's version of the American Dream.
After war has been declared, before he joins the I & R platoon,
he goes to a special meeting and hears the following speech:

> All right, we're in a war, men, the speaker says, we gotta
> fight for the country, but we don't want to be forgettin' our
> private enemies. He pounds the speaker's table over which
> a flag with a cross is spread. There's the foreign element we
> got to get rid of, that are conspiring to take over the
> country. There are cheers from the hundred men seated in
> camp chairs. We gotta stick together, or we'll be havin' our
> women raped, and the Red Hammer of Red Jew Fascist
> Russia WILL BE SMASHING YOUR DOOR DOWN
> . . . Who takes away your jobs, who tries to sneak up on
> your wives and your daughters and even your mothers
> 'cause they wouldn't stop at nothing, who's out to get
> YOU and YOU 'cause you ain't a Red and a Jew, and you
> don' wanta bow down before a filthy goddam no-good
> Communist who don't respect the Lord's name, and
> would stop at nothing.
> Let's kill them! Gallagher shrieks. He is shaking with
> excitement. That's it men, we're gonna clean up on 'em,

after the war we're really gonna have an organisation, I got telegrams here from our com-*pat*-riots, patriots as well as friends, and they're all sticking with us. You're all in on the ground floor, men, and those of ya that are goin' into the army gotta learn to use your weapons so that afterward . . . afterward . . . You get the idea men. We ain't licked, we're getting bigger all the time.[4]

Mailer's warning about the dangers of impending fascism in America does not rest on characters like Cummings with their intellectual commitment to fascism. Cummings' confident prediction that 'the army . . . is a preview of the future'[5] gains its force within the novel from the portraits of Gallagher, Brown, etc., in pre-war America. Cummings understands the importance of such elements as his response to Lieutenant Colonel Conn shows; he calls the anti-semitic, anti-Negro, anti-union views of Conn a 'kind of filth' but adds to Hearn his opinion that 'he is more nearly right than you suspect.'[6] The prejudices and fears of Conn and Gallagher can be exploited to advance the 'power-morality' in post-war America; the lumpen proletariat and the fears and philistinism of certain sections of the bourgeoisie are, Mailer suggests, the backbone of political reaction. Cummings and Croft represent the potential leadership of this kind of reaction, for both are capable, courageous and resolutely authoritarian. As with the other characters, the 'Time Machine' device is used to relate their personal qualities to their economic, social and sexual history. Whilst Mount Anaka is used to symbolise what they have in common, their characters are nicely differentiated to suggest their different levels of political consciousness and their different spheres of action. Croft is a man of practical activity, expressing a fearless, unselfconscious desire for power:

Leading the men was a responsibility he craved; he felt powerful and certain at such moments. He longed to be in the battle . . .[7]

Cummings on the other hand, is the theoretical exponent of the power principle and his views, appropriately enough, are presented through his notebook and in two major exchanges with Hearn. He holds that since men are manifestly *not* equal, and since man's greatest achievements have been based on this fact, it is an irrelevance to concern oneself with democratic ideals – society must be structured so that civilisation can advance as quickly and as far as possible. There are similarities between Cummings' beliefs and those of Gerald Crich, the streamlining capitalist in *Women in Love*: both see the mass as instrumental to a great dream of 'progress'. Democracy and egalitarian societies are inefficient and obstruct social progress and for this reason Cummings admires Hitler's beliefs and confidently predicts that America, with all her resources, can take over and realise the German Dream. The 'fear-ladder' which is the structure of the army is efficient and America after the war will take it as its model:

> America is going to absorb that dream, it's in the business of doing it now. When you've created power, materials, armies, they don't wither of their own accord. Our vacuum as a nation is filled with released power, and I can tell you that we're out of the backwaters of history now.[8]

Although in his talks with Hearn he concentrates on the 'dream' and on 'history' and the individual's subordination to it, from his notebooks we learn that his own desire is to 'mould the curve'[9], not to serve it. His is a 'peculiarly American'[10] brand of fascism, combining individualism and idealism with a dream of totalitarianism.

The political position represented by Cummings and Croft is presented as powerful and even attractive* in certain respects. In the war, the Thoreauvian individualism of Valsen and the liberalism of Hearn cannot withstand it and the implication, clearly, is that they could not withstand it in peacetime either. There is in fact, some ambiguity in the novel as to what forces could oppose it. Croft is finally defeated by the collective resistance of the platoon in throwing away their kit, making it impossible to continue to the peak of the mountain. Similarly, the Japanese forces collapse before Cummings' master plan can be put into action and the army achieves victory in his absence.

---

* Again Mailer's comment in *The Presidential Papers* comes to mind, that 'Beneath the ideology in *The Naked and the Dead* was an obsession with violence. The characters for whom I had most secret admiration, like Croft, were violent people.' (p. 149)

These two reversals mirror each other, as their two triumphs over Hearn and Valsen, had done earlier. And at the end of the novel two new elements – the inertia of the masses and bureaucracy – have moved to the centre of the political debate.

If there is a force to oppose the threat from the Right, it may lie in the collectivity of the enlisted men – symbolised as a parabola in Cummings' notebook:

The men resisted him, resisted change, with maddening inertia. No matter how you pushed them, they always gave ground sullenly, regrouped once the pressure was off.[11]

The men in the platoon, 'helpless and corrupt'* though they are throughout the novel, finally defeat Croft; it is not the hornets' nest nor the heights of Mount Anarka that stop him but the men's understanding that together they possess enough power to oppose him:

Dimly they sensed that if they threw away enough possessions they would not be able to continue the patrol . . .[12]

Nor is it Valsen who gives momentum to this action, but Polack, who by shouting that the hornets are in pursuit, has the wit to see and use the opportunity. Neither the liberal Hearn nor the self-conscious rebel stages this revolt against Croft; it is the collective action of the 'masses' led by the opportunist who feels at a particular moment that it is his interest to take such action. This is not, clearly, a Marxist position.

Similarly, it is the despised bureaucrat Major Dalleson and not General Cummings who successfully completes the occupation of the island and the novel ends with Dalleson at his desk contentedly planning the details of a new training programme and thinking up a teaching aid in the form of a pin-up photograph overlaid with the co-ordinate grid system. The future, these paragraphs suggest, lies neither with the liberal nor the

* 'People say it is a novel without hope. Actually it offers a good deal of hope. I intended it to be a parable about the movement of man through history. I tried to explore the outrageous propositions of cause and effect, of effort and recompense, in a sick society. The book finds man corrupted, confused to the point of helplessness, but it also finds that there are limits beyond which he cannot be pushed, and it finds that even in his corruption and sickness there are yearnings for a better world.' Mailer in an interview in *The New Yorker* (23 Oct 1948).

idealistic fascist, but with the bureaucrat, the *apparatchik*. The army may be a preview of a future American society but not as in the heroic conception of Cummings but in the form of a mediocre bureaucracy administered by Dalleson. He and not the general is ideally suited to survive and prosper in such a system because he already experiences himself as an instrument of the system (the army or the state in peacetime) and gets his greatest pleasure from the thought that he can operate or even facilitate its processes. Thus, although the main part of the novel focuses on the conflict between liberalism and elitism both are invalidated by the working-out of the action. And although the novel may be called Marxist in the stress it places on social conditioning, the specific concern with American capitalism and fascism shifts, in the closing pages, to the dangers of totalitarianism (a quite different concept), where, as Cummings bitterly suggests, 'it would be the hacks who would occupy history's seat after the war'.[13]

The political problems raised in *The Naked and the Dead* in the larger framework of the Pacific war, are present in his second novel, but the focus in *Barbary Shore* is narrower and more intensive and there is a greater political specificity. The danger of totalitarianism is the main preoccupation, and this provides the allegorical frame within which a political debate about revolutionary socialism (Trotskyism) and Stalinism is enacted; the issue at stake is the possibility of a radical political solution to the problem of America. The action takes place almost entirely in a small boarding house in Brooklyn, during the cold-war period in America and after the betrayal of 'the greatest event in man's history'[14] – the Russian Revolution of 1917. The political argument which emerges from this discussion can be crudely summarised as follows: once the revolutionary doctrine of Marxism offered liberation, equality and sanity to mankind – 'the dream in all its purity'[15] as Lovett called it – but after Lenin's death, the visionary Trotskyists gave up power to the Stalinist bureaucrats of the Soviet Union; the revolutionary potential was contained with the concept of socialism in one country and revolutionary internationalism betrayed in the interests of Soviet foreign policy.

The historical function of La Sovietica is to destroy the intellectual content of Marxism.[16]

This much emerges in the confession-interrogation sessions between McLeod, the revolutionary turned Stalinist 'hack', and Hollingsworth, an agent for the national security organisation closely resembling the FBI. McLeod's personal history is used to examine the history of revolutionary socialism. Set against the reconstruction of McLeod's part in the purges and labour-camps of the twenties and thirties, are Lovett's fantasied images of the Revolution as he discovers his own revolutionary past. The hopes and ideals of the young (Trotskyist) revolutionary contrast sharply with the list of Stalinist betrayals:

> Of all the students in the study group, none could have been more ardent than I, and for a winter and a spring, I lived more intensely in the past than I could ever in the present, until the sight of a policeman on his mount became the Petrograd proletariat crawling to fame between the legs of a Cossack's horse . . . There was never a revolution to equal it, and never a city more glorious than Petrograd, and for all that period of my life I lived another and braved the ice of winter and the summer flies in Vyborg while across my adopted country of the past, winds of the revolution blew their flame, and all of us suffered hunger while we drank at the wine of equality, and knew with what passion to be buried that our revolution would beget others . . .*

Lovett's amnesia is the symbol of his alienation from the socialist movement but by the end of the novel, he has at least recovered something of the revolutionary spirit – enough to inherit the 'little object' and the 'remnants of my (McLeod's) socialist culture'.[17] Lovett and Lannie Madison are presented as the split halves of modern political consciousness and their sterile love-making underlines this split. In Lannie we get an image of pathological alienation. Literally driven mad by the murder of Trotsky, she has spent the time since 1939 in various institutions, being given ECT treatment and escaping her last

---

* *Barbary Shore*, p. 224. This interpretation is basically that of Trotsky in his *History of the Russian Revolution*, and the images of Vyborg and the cossack horses are from the same source. Similarly, the emphasis on the Stalinists' bureaucratism is taken from Trotsky's *New Course* – particularly the chapters on NEP and Bureaucratism.

clinic only to become embroiled in the Hollingworth–McLeod confrontation. After this, she kills her 'mouse', paints her room black and is led away to yet another institution. Her presence contributes significantly to McLeod's surrender to Hollingsworth – 'it was you and not him who wore me down',[18] and she embodies the effects of the betrayal on the socialist movement – confusion, defeat, and final madness. Her vision of the new state (which is in fact shared by McLeod) as a gigantic concentration camp complete with brainwashing techniques, torture and mass deaths, suggests the despair of the radical of making a real revolution in America or elsewhere.

This pessimistic vision is supported by the triumph, allegorically, of totalitarianism – the departure 'To the ends of the earth. To Barbary'[19] by Hollingsworth and Guinivere. As a political symbol Guinivere stands for the American proletariat, seduced by materialistic desires and the ideology of mass entertainment, and ignorant of political doctrine – 'I don't know anything about politics'.[20] She embodies the energy and the 'inertia' of the masses; each of the boarders needs her for his own ends and no system can succeed without her. Her failed marriage to McLeod suggests the failure to bring Marxism into meaningful relationship with the American working class, and she rejects his plea to continue the attempt:

> I'm your bloody salvation, that's all.[21]

Her alliance with Hollingsworth and their departure to Barbary is Mailer's metaphor for the shift to an authoritarian dictatorship of the future:

> 'Will you always tell me what to do?' His voice was balm and I could sense her drawing strength. 'I will tell you what to do. Over and over I will tell you what to do.'[22]

In political terms: the centralised state will absorb the energies of the masses and liberalism, socialism and democratic capitalism will give way to totalitarianism.

Towards the end the novel, as Mailer commented in *Advertisements for Myself*, 'collapsed into a chapter of political speech and never quite recovered'.[23] This failure can be attributed to two main problems: first the intransigent nature of the political issues raised in *Barbary Shore* and, objectively, the unavailibility of a radical political solution to those issues. Secondly, the political preoccupations were, I think, attended by great intellectual excitement but insufficient imaginative commitment. It has been generally recognised how important this failure was to Mailer's literary achievement in *Barbary Shore* but it was, I think, also a crucial moment in his political thinking. Although the discussion of the Russian Revolution in *Barbary Shore* is couched in fairly orthodox Trotskyist terms, there is another, quite different, viewpoint informing the indictment. Mailer felt that the Russian Revolution, the revolution of our time, had failed because whatever else it had done, it had not abolished the State (i.e. authority) and so had not made a revolution in the consciousness of the Russian people.

Mailer came to this conclusion slowly and only after he had written *The Naked and the Dead*, and it was the main cause for his break with the Progressive Party in 1949. It undermined his belief that organised politics and the redistribution of material wealth would ever bring about the kinds of changes that he, Mailer, thought necessary. But, as can be seen in this his second novel, this distrust of the Soviet system was intimately connected with a similar* and in many ways, deeper distrust, of the United States. This was because Mailer did not approach either system as a Marxist (even a Trotskyist Marxist) but as an anarchist: the issue was not for him primarily that of the class struggle and economic exploitation but that of the individual, freedom, and growth within the centralised state. McLeod's speech in the twenty-ninth chapter of *Barbary Shore* argues that war and preparations for war were turning both America and Russia into unfree societies, that the dynamics of a war economy will lead inevitably to destruction. America and the Soviet Union become more and more alike as they become increasingly irrational and *this* is the 'drift into barbarism' which Mailer warns against.

The concept of totalitarianism which shapes McLeod's

* At the Mount Holyoke debate in 1952, Mailer with Dwight Macdonald and many others debated the merits and demerits of the West (American capitalism) and the East (Soviet communism). MacDonald, another radical and ex-Trotskyist, chose the West, whereas Mailer took an 'I can't choose' position on the grounds that there was little to choose between one kind of totalitarianism and another. 'The Meaning of Western Defence', N. Mailer, *Dissent* (Spring 1954).

thinking and Lannie's image of the future and which was to dominate Mailer's political thinking for the next two decades, became a catchword among American intellectuals of the fifties. Because it is so important in Mailer's writing of this period, it is worth considering it in its historical context of American politics generally. 'Totalitarianism' was seen as the result of state power directed towards a single ideological position and after the revelations of Stalinist authoritarianism, many American intellectual radicals became hostile to ideology as such. For some, 'the end of ideology'[24] was used to mean the end of class struggle; the modification of late capitalism by welfare legislation, redistribution taxation, the consolidation of powerful unions and an acceptance by all political parties of Keynesian full employment policies made such a struggle seem unnecessary. American society was seen as composed of different interest groups with competing interests but not as a class society as it was in the thirties. In this climate, the threat was seen not from the Right or Left but from the Centralised State and many radicals responded with admiration to the three seminal works on totalitarianism: Hannah Arendt's *Origins of Totalitarianism*, Orwell's *1984*, and Milosz's *The Captive Mind*. Cultural criticism – complaints about standardisation, political conformism and cultural mediocrity – replaced truly political criticism on the American Left. Mass culture, unlike economic exploitation and racial discrimination, is not obviously susceptible to correction by political means, so campaigns against it were hardly continuous with the older radicalism. Moreover, critics of mass culture borrowed many of their themes from European aristocratic and romantic reactionaries, and the result was often extremely ambiguous in its political implications.

This trend among American radicals in the early fifties undoubtedly had an effect on Mailer's political development; it led him away from the direct concern with ideological issues such as one finds in *The Naked and the Dead* and *Barbary Shore*, and whilst he never repudiated Marx or Marxism, as did many American radicals, he attempted a fusion with many of the new elements of the fifties. The best comment on this process is his own, made in an interview in 1955, and reprinted in *Advertisements for Myself*:

Q. How has your social ken changed since you wrote *The Naked and the Dead*?

A. I was an anarchist then, and I'm an anarchist today. In between I belonged to the Progressive Party during the Wallace campaign, and then broke off rather abruptly at the time of the Waldorf Peace Conference in 1949. What followed was a period of political wandering in the small circle of libertarian socialism. I was at the same time very radical and yet half-hearted about it. I've also been a contributing editor on 'Dissent'. Still am of course . . . Let me put it that today I'm a Marxian anarchist, which is a contradiction in terms, but not an unprofitable contradiction for trying to do some original thinking. I suppose part of the change in my 'social ken' is *that politics as politics interests me less today than politics as part of everything else in life*.[25]

In *The Deer Park* Mailer does just this; he treats politics as 'part of everything else in life' and examines the effects of totalitarianism on sexuality and creative work in the capital of cinema and its 'playground', Desert D'Or, alias Palm Springs. The novel is in fact culture-criticism in a fairly direct way. The distorting nature of mass entertainment and commercial values, touched on in the portrait of Guinivere in *Barbary Shore*, is tracked to its *source*: hence the choice of locale. Hollywood is seen as an ideology factory, producing the cold-war patriotism and the sentimental, escapist myths about sex, relationships and reality which dominate American consciousness. This, it is suggested, is the other face of totalitarianism; State repression can take the form of concentration camps with guards and physical coercion, or it can exist in a more insidious form at the ideological level of the mass media. In the preface to *The Deer Park* Mailer quotes from Mouffle D'Angerville's account of Louis XV's Deer Park to underline the point about 'the evil which this dreadful place did to the morals of the people'.

The characters at Desert D'Or apparently have a greater degree of individual liberty, sexual license and freedom from economic want than the inhabitants of any other place in America, yet, the novel suggests, all this, like so much else in Desert D'Or, is an illusion. From the very first chapter the disparity between appearance and reality in the town is stressed:

It was a town built out of no other obvious motive than commercial profit and so no sign of commerce was allowed to appear. Desert D'Or was without a main street, and its stores looked like anything but stores.[26]

In the scenes featuring Herman Teppis we are shown how behind the friendly, co-operative facade at Supreme Pictures, lies a rigidly authoritarian business organisation whose manipulation of its 'staff' extends beyond the screen to their personal lives. But Supreme Pictures is not merely an internally authoritarian organisation producing films with a pernicious ideological content; it is also integrally linked to the repressive McCarthyist politics of the State, as is made clear through its co-operation with the Subversive Committee in Congress and its refusal to employ Eitel until he conforms to their political line.

Eitel's rebellion and his eventual capitulation is the centrepiece of Mailer's picture of this world. His political nonconformity is structurally linked to his possibilities as a writer and artist which are, in turn, closely related to his ability to 'love'. His defeat in the 'unjust world',[27] when it happens, occurs on all three levels. Where his original statement to the Committee includes his opinion that 'Patriotism is for pigs',[28] his capitulatory statement which will allow him to produce a prostituted version of his script, contains the usual formulae of 'totalitarian' patriotism:

. . . recognise the useful and patriotic function of the Committee, and I testify today without duress, proud to be able to contribute my share to the defence of this country against all infiltration and subversion.[29]

Where his original version of 'Saints and Lovers' was conceived as an *exposé* of the romance between totalitarianism and sentimentality in the mass media, the completed script is merely another contribution to that romance. With his love affair with Elena Esposito which at one time represented a qualitative break with the marriages and affairs of the past, he betrays this possibility and settles for being 'not unhappy'[30] and having a 'bedroom better than most'.[31] The conclusion, it seems, is that there is more than one form of 'duress' and Eitel's defeat as a man and an artist serves as a coda for Mailer's belief that politics is 'a part of everything else'.

Faye and O'Shaughnessy also, of course, illustrate this belief but are intended to suggest the ways in which the totalitarian world can be opposed. O'Shaughnessy defies the FBI men when they come, breaks with Lulu Meyers and refuses a job in Hollywood, thus living out his radicalism at the personal as well as the narrowly political level. Faye's life also embodies his beliefs – both political and philosophical. They are both (as was suggested in my first chapter) essays in the existential hero, pre-hipsters, created in response to Mailer's political view of America; their defining characteristics, *courage, instinct*, and a certain kind of *power*, are what enable them to survive uncompromised in what Mailer in 'The White Negro' calls 'l'univers concentrationnaire'.[32] In the opening statement of *Advertisements for Myself* Mailer outlines these positives – with some additions – in an explicit way:

> So, yes, it may be the time to say that the Republic is in real peril, and we are the cowards who must defend courage, sex, consciousness, the beatuty of the body, the search for love, and the capture of what may be, after all, an heroic destiny.[33]

It is all here: the rage at the state of the 'Republic', the appeal to the passional life, the dependence on minimal physical verities which are not identified with any specific political cause or principle. They are to be rescued from annihilation by the totalitarian state and so their value is asserted abstractly, without any political context. Mailer in this passage conveniently ignores the fact that a 'totalitarian' state could well celebrate some form of courage, sex, the beauty of the body, etc., without in the least changing its fundamental character – as Hannah Arendt's researches into Nazi Germany have shown.[34] One of the difficulties in describing his political position in this period is that he defines 'totalitarianism' in a variety of ways, expanding it to include things he finds objectionable for very different reasons; pacifists, liberals, modern architecture, Hollywood, experimental theatre, homosexuals, masturbation, David Reisman and beatniks are all at different times included under the general heading 'totalitarian' or likely to reinforce totalitarianism. This confusion of levels is in part a result of his thesis that

politics is 'a part of everything else in life', but it robs the term of
any firm political significance, reducing it to the level of an emo-
tive catchword. It is even more important therefore to examine
the positives he puts forward.

Conceiving of life as a battle against 'totalitarianism', Mailer
returns to the combat virtue of courage, following Hemingway
in making this rather secondary virtue the centre of his moral
and intellectual universe. (The militaristic conception of politics and culture is visible throughout the imagery of *Advertisements for Myself* and *The Presidential Papers*.) In an article in
Dissent (Fall 1956) writing about 'the Tragedy of Parris Island'
Mailer took the opportunity to make a general defence of courage:

> . . . our generation of sensitive people has begun to deny the
> proper existence of such virtues as courage, and I would
> declare this to be one of the abuses of psychoanalysis . . . the
> new faith can strip from anyone exactly their most striking
> and admirable human qualities.

In this statement he goes back not merely to Hemingway, but to
an earlier tradition that Hemingway attacked in his statement
in *A Farewell to Arms*:

> Abstract words such as glory, honour, courage or hallow
> were obscene beside the concrete names of villages, the
> numbers of roads . . . etc.

Yet throughout *Advertisements for Myself*, and particularly in
'The White Negro', Mailer celebrates courage and 'instinct'
for their own sake, in the 'abstract'. Behind this celebration
lies his fear of totalitarianism: the state, with the mass media
at its command, has invaded every aspect of conscious life; instincts escape this influence and are God-given, and it is in
them therefore that Mailer puts his trust. The 'imperatives of
the self' are what he clings to in the absence of feasible imperatives of an earlier kind. It is a classical retreat from ideology
which, I would argue, is only an ideological position of
another, basically conservative, kind.

In response to Jean Malaquais' attack on 'The White
Negro' on roughly the same ground, Mailer admits his political desperation and his political hopes and places them in

precise historical framework:

> The growth of human consciousness in this century de-
> manded — for its expanding vitality — that a revolution be
> made, that a mankind be liberated, and since the attempt
> failed in its frontal revolutionary attack, failed precisely to
> change the exploitative character of our productive relations,
> it may well be that the rise of the hipster represents the first
> wind of a second revolution in this century, moving not
> forward towards action and more rational equitable dis-
> tribution, but backward towards being and the secrets of
> human energy, not forward to the collectivity which was
> totalitarian in the proof but backward to the nihilism of
> creative adventurers, a revolution admittedly impossible to
> conceive even in its outlines . . .[35]

'The White Negro' as a political document is an admission of
Mailer's despair about a socialist revolution (despite his claim
to be still a 'Marxian anarchist') and about his attempt to imagine the outlines of the second revolution which he admits is
'impossible to conceive'. The hipster he conceives is, as Malaquais says, 'a gorgeous flower of Mailer's romantic idealism'.[36]

Mailer's fascination with the 'secrets of human energy', or vitality, or power, had been present throughout his writing, as
both Norman Podhoretz and James Baldwin have observed,[37]
but it was not until the mid-fifties that he began to equate morality with power, or as he puts it in 'The White Negro', health
with energy. This obsession can be partly explained by
Mailer's feelings of helplessness and irrelevance within American politics, which he refers to in *Advertisements for Myself*, and
by the impotence of the American Left generally during the
Dulles–Eisenhower–McCarthy period. It also represents his
attempt to find instances of power at the individual level to
oppose the power of the state. The result in his fiction is a preoccupation with the type of non-victim, the all-powerful man, the
maker of conditions who brings his courage and his instinct to
bear on his situation — and this preoccupation culminates in the
creation of Rojack in *An American Dream*. The concern with
power, itself the result of feelings of political impotence, had a
distinct political influence on Mailer's other attitudes. Classic
liberalism was no longer a bulwark of freedom, for it was

defused and powerless in the 'totalitarian' state. The liberals, by their attempts to eliminate differences between men – because of their faith in linear progress, psychoanalysis and environmentalism – are in fact constricting the areas of human possibility. Mailer maintained his dislike for patriotic reactionaries and ex-radical anti-Communists, but his impatience with liberalism, especially liberal academics, became almost as strong during this period. The liberal acceptance of psychoanalysis was particularly dangerous, since in Mailer's view, psychoanalysis was a tool of American ideology, used to reduce the resistance within the totalitarian society—to tame the power of the rebel with Milltown.

At the end of *The Deer Park*, Elena Esposito is shown resisting her analyst's efforts to adjust her to the goals of social and financial success. In *Advertisements for Myself* (in the story 'The Man Who studied Yoga') Mailer realises his hostility to psycoanalysis in a brilliant parody of its effects. The Slovoda family relationships are reduced to comic banality by the ways in which they use (or misuse) psychoanalytical jargon to talk about their feelings and friends. But Mailer reveals the key to his political objections in the conversation between Sam Slovoda and his analyst Dr Sergius. In a discussion of his past radicalism, Sam resists the implication that social protest or criticism can be treated as psychological maladjustment:

> Sam will argue with Sergius but it is very difficult. He will say, 'Perhaps you sneer at radicals because it is more comfortable to ignore such ideas. Once you became interested it might introduce certain unpleasant changes in your life.'
>
> 'Why,' says Sergius, 'do you feel it so necessary to assume that I am a bourgeois interested only in my comfort?'
>
> 'How can I express these things,' says Sam, 'if you insist that my opinions are the expression of neurotic needs, and your opinions are merely dispassionate medical advice?'[38]

In this exchange, Mailer pinpoints the anomaly of psychoanalytic practice – it has taken from medicine the traditional doctor–patient relationship without a valid basis for doing so. The authority of the doctor in the medical situation is legitimate because it rests on the scientific knowledge of the doctor. In the psychoanalytic situation, there is no scientific basis by

which the analyst's views of reality and politics is more valid
than that of the patient. Mailer dramatises the point, in a story
written in 1952, which has subsequently been treated in the
writings of Laing and other modern psychological theorists.

Mailer's hostility towards psychoanalysis stems from his fear
of its possible application in a totalitarian state, but he is not
content to point out this danger, he goes on to reject psychoanalysis totally.* This can be seen in many of the essays in *Advertisements for Myself, Presidential Papers* and *Cannibals and Christians*,
in the portrait of the TV producer in *An American Dream*, and in
the sessions between DJ's mother and her analyst, nicknamed
Dr Fixit, in *Why are We in Vietnam?* The reasons behind his
wholesale rejection of psychoanalysis lie in his reactionary
notion that instinct is more 'authentic' than socially acquired
behaviour, and the treatment of sex and violence in his work
can be understood only in this light. The Slovodas and their
friends repress their excitement at the pornographic movie by
talking and joking about it:

> They begin to discuss the film. As intelligent people they
> must dominate it. Someone wonders about the actors in the
> piece, and the discussion begins afresh. 'I fail to see,' says
> Louise, 'why they should be so hard to classify. Pornography
> is a job to the criminal and prostitute elements.'[39]

Mailer satirises how 'intelligent people' intellectualise experience that could, and he suggests *should*, be dealt with at another
level. It is not merely the limitations of their discussions (the
cliches and pseudo-sociological classifications) that he attacks,
but the fact that they discuss it *at all*. It would be more honest
and authentic, he implies, if they were to 'perform the orgy that
tickles at the heart of their desires'.[40] His treatment of violence

* For a very appropriate comment on this attitude, see Susan Sontag's
Against Interpretation:

> But the disenchantment of American intellectuals with psychoanalytic
> ideas, as with the earlier disenchantment with Marxist ideas (a parallel
> case) is premature. Marxism is not Stalinism or the suppression of the
> Hungarian revolution; psychoanalysis is not the Park Avenue analyst or
> the psychoanalytic journals or the suburban matron discussing her child's
> Oedipus complex. Disenchantment is the characteristic posture of contem-
> porary American intellectuals, but disenchantment is often the product of
> laziness. We are not tenacious enough about ideas, as we have not been
> serious or honest enough about sexuality. (p. 258)

in *An American Dream* and *Why are We in Vietnam?* is informed by the same principle; specific and authentic acts of violence, executed by the instinctive but sane individual are proper whereas violence which is 'large-scale and abstract'[41] is not. A few days before the incident in which Mailer stabbed his wife in 1960 he gave an interview (later printed in *Mademoiselle*, February 1961) in which he uses Orwell's image of the heel in the face of the dying man:

> *Mailer*: If you are going to grind your heel into the face of a dying man, I still insist on the authority of my existential logic: let the act finally be authentic. If you're going to do it, *do it*.

> *Interviewer*: You mean enjoy it?

> *Mailer*: The poor soul is going out of existence. You might as well enjoy yourself! If you're going to grind your boot in his face don't do it with the feeling, 'I'm horrible, I'm psychotic, I should be in the bughouse.' Do it.

The justification is partly a psychological one, of release from tension, an overcoming of the deepest social taboos to define the reality of the individual's 'imperatives of the self' *against* his social existence. Guilty suppression, sublimation, and rationalisation – all socially acquired forms of control – are all equally inauthentic in Mailer's terms.

Clearly such a psychological theory has considerable political implications which Mailer, as a 'Marxian anarchist' (or a 'libertarian socialist' as he defines himself elsewhere) cannot follow through. The theory that given certain murderous or rapist impulses the only 'brave' response is to admit that they are there and to act them out, is determinist and therefore totally incompatible with a Marxist or socialist view of human nature. 'Instinct' is used throughout 'The White Negro' and in *An American Dream* and in *Why are We in Vietnam?* without any attempt at intellectual or biological precision; the impulse to grind one's heel in the face of a dying man, or to murder and create for that matter, are of course anything but primitive instincts, they are culturally determined modes of behaviour. Even granting a sexual and a survival instinct in man, the form in which these instincts express themselves is conditioned by the social situation – as Mailer dramatised so successfully in *The Naked and The Dead*. Thus despite his determination to make a 'revolution in the consciousness of our time',[42] his political thinking is characterised by confusion and eclecticism. Isolated from any political movement, Mailer attempts to support his totalitarian-instinct thesis with the language of Sartre and Kierkegaard, but too often reduces existential concepts to the repetition of words like Being, Time and Dread, divorced from any context or meaning. In 'The White Negro' he borrows many of the ideas of Wilhelm Reich to expound his idea of the hipster and the regenerative power of the orgasm, but this leads him into the same mystification about 'energy' as it did Reich himself. The essays in *The Presidential Papers* and *Cannibals and Christians* also indicate a return to nineteenth-century radicalism, where in the mechanical-organic tradition Mailer finds parallels for his ideas on both totalitarianism and instinctivism.

Two metaphors – the professional-amateur and the disease-physician – introduced in the 'Prefatory Paper' provide the key to Mailer's political thinking in these essays. He writes of the problems of twentieth-century America like an eighteenth- or nineteenth-century radical. The professional-amateur dichotomy belongs to a period of absolute monarchy in which the role of 'court wit'[43] or inspired fool may have been valid, but it proves inadequate basis for writing about the cold war, Vietnam, the Cuban crisis and other political issues of his own time. Mailer's objections to professionalism have a historical precedent in the writing of Edmund Burke, a debt which he acknowledges in *Cannibals and Christians* in a quotation from Burke's *Reflections on the Revolution in France*:

> When men are too much confined to professional and faculty habits, and as it were inveterate in the recurrent employment of that narrow circle, they are rather disabled than qualified for whatever depends on the knowledge of mankind, on experience of mixed affairs, on a comprehensive, connected view of the various, complicated, external and internal interests, which go to the formation of that multifarious thing called a state.[44]

The second metaphorical model is that of America as the sick organism with Mailer as the prescribing physician with a 'comprehensive, connected view'. Disease, plague, cancer and sickness are consistently used to refer to American conditions. The objective of the physician-amateur is to return the patient to health, to 'organic' wholeness:

> Politics is like a body of organs. When the body is sick, it is usually because one or another organ has become too weak or too powerful in its function. If the disproportion is acute, a war goes on in the body, an inflammatory sickness, a fever, a crisis. The war decided, the organ subsides, different in size, stronger or weaker, it returns to its part of the body's function . . . Acute diseases are like political forces personified by heroes. And slack diseases, featureless, symptomless diseases like virus and colds and the ubiquitous cancer, are the appropriate metaphor of all those political forces like the FBI, or like the liberalism of the Democratic Party, which are historically faceless.[45]

With this statement Mailer returns to the nineteenth-century organic view of society – a tradition of nineteenth-century radicalism in which political distinctions of Left and Right have no place (which in the twentieth century has influenced writers as diverse as Lawrence and Orwell). Burke, whom Mailer cites several times in *Cannibals and Christians*, was the last thinker who could find the 'organic' in existing society.* As the new industrial society established itself, later social critics like Carlyle and Ruskin could find their organic image only in the past, hence their medievalism.

Mailer it seems to me idealises the eighteenth and nineteenth centuries much in the way that social thinkers of the nineteenth century idealised the medieval period. He identifies his objections to mass society, which he calls totalitarianism, with their criticisms of the mechanical, industrial society. His objection to the *misuse* of science and technology at times becomes a hostility

---

* The organic conception of society, stressing interrelation and interdependence of the whole social organism, grew up in opposition to a *laissez-faire* system, but also in opposition to a mechanical, atomic notion of equality. It was used as one point in the attack on the conditions of men in industrial production where the 'cash-nexus' was the only active relation between men, and as such had some kind of radical impetus. See Raymond Williams, *Culture and Society* p. 145–6.

towards technology as such, and he rails at 'florescent lighting' and 'air-conditioners',[46] for example. Further, his distrust of 'totalitarian' rationality leads him close to a rejection of rationality as such, and at such moments he resembles a kind of intellectual Luddite. Although the targets Mailer attacks in his paper on 'Totalitarianism' are often arbitrary they have the force of being concrete. The alternatives to totalitarianism, on the other hand, remain the vaguest of abstractions. His positives are presented not in terms of an alternative society but in terms of individual experience:

> The essence of totalitarianism is that it beheads. It beheads individuality, variety, dissent, extreme possibility, romantic faith, it blinds vision, deadens instinct, it obliterates the past.[47]

'Vision', 'instincts', and 'the past' raise more questions than they answer; whose vision, past and instincts are to be maintained in America? ('Whose vision will prevail?'[48] is precisely the question Mailer asks when confronted by Lyndon B. Johnson's rhetorical use of the word vision.) The medievalism of the nineteenth-century romantics, although it was a 'false past' in many ways, represented a much more substantial and detailed image of a possible alternative society. In failing to concretise the organic side of his metaphor, Mailer offers no 'comprehensive, connected view' but is thrown back on his own romantic anarchism.

This failure is noticeable in his treatment of American culture, but it is even more striking when he attempts to discuss specific political events – as he does in his paper on 'Foreign Affairs' in *The Presidential Papers* and in the essays on Vietnam in *Cannibals and Christians*. With no coherent political concepts, save his thesis on totalitarianism and instinctivism, Mailer in effect reduces the complexities of international politics to the level of personalities involved. That Krushchev and Kennedy may be 'half-way decent as men'[49] and whether Kennedy has a good or a 'dull' imagination are marginal if not completely irrelevant to a discussion of the Bay of Pigs invasion. Mailer's comments where they are not merely inaccurate and ill-informed, are politically naive and volunterist. In the 'Letter to Fidel Castro', he opens with a résumé of Castro's landing near

Niquero and the guerrillas' fight with Batista's army; he goes
on to express his admiration for Castro's military successes and
the eventual capture of Havana in the following terms:

> It was not unheroic. Truth, it was worthy of Cortes. It was as
> if the ghost of Cortes had appeared in our century riding
> Zapata's white horse. You were the first and greatest hero to
> appear in the world since the Second War.[50]

The political inappropriateness of the comparison is glaringly
obvious – and there is, apparently, no ironic intention. The
idealist liberator turned Communist is compared with the
Spanish conquistador whose brutal and brutalising search for
gold and converts was one of the first examples of the colonial
exploitation from which Cuba suffered right up to the time of
the Batista regime. He then draws on the legend of the Mexican
revolutionary and his white horse – which became a symbol of
the revolutionary struggle against colonial oppression. To imagine the ghost of Cortes* riding Zapata's horse is itself a gross
contradiction in terms; Castro, Cortes and Zapata are all vul-
garly lumped together as examples of Latin American heroes.
What Mailer is saluting is, again, the virtue of 'courage' and he
subsumes all political distinctions in his obsession with this
quality.

Mailer then proceeds to explain Cuba's subsequent political
development and her relations with America and the Soviet
Union:

> Now, at the moment, revolted by the cheap muck of the most
> cess-filled brains in our land, disheartened by the impossi-
> bility of receiving a fair report from us, you are obviously get-
> ting ready to commit your political fortune to Krushchev.[51]

Again, personalities and rhetoric are substituted for political
analysis; this statement is an arrant projection of Mailer's own
feelings about America. The sense of a mind less and less able to
distinguish between its own obsessions and external realities,
which was intermittant in *Advertisements for Myself*, is almost
overwhelming here. One does not need to know the 'statistics'†

* It seems possible that Mailer knows Cortes only as the mythologised 'stout
Cortez' of Keats' poem – and that he shares the nineteenth-century poetic
view of him.

† In the first paper, entitled 'Heroes and Leaders', Mailer admitted that *The*

of the situation to know that Cuba's alliance with the Communist bloc was forced on her, at the economic level, by the American blockade on Cuban sugar and her refusal to export foodstuffs to Cuba. Castro, in fact, repeatedly negotiated for a market for sugar with the 'most cess-filled brains in our land' and with other Western countries, before accepting a trade alliance and political ties with the USSR. Whilst other Left intellectuals including the writers in *Dissent* (of which Mailer was still an editorial board member) are debating whether American governmental policy accelerated Cuba's development towards a socialist form of government, Mailer ignores the reality of such economic and political factors. Cuba's ties with the USSR are explained in terms of interpersonal friendship:

> You have a new friend. He (Krushchev) was good to you at a time when my country promulgated its disgrace. You are Latin. Your honour is to be loyal. Still, I must say, that as one of your sympathizers I do not trust your new friend. He is a wise peasant bully.[52]

Behind this moralistic terminology ('disgrace', 'honour', 'loyal' and 'bully') lie Mailer's political objections to Stalinism and to political 'hacks' like Krushchev, but the absence of any specifically *political* language is typical of much of his writing of this period. It reflects, I think, a special kind of isolation and privatisation. His own inability to find a political reference group in the late fifties and early sixties is also reflected in his irascible dismissal of existing groups and their activities. In an interview with Paul Krassner in the sixth paper, Mailer describes the Peace Movement as 'totalitarian' on the grounds that it is now a conventional organisation:

> *Mailer*: It's too safe. That's the thing I don't like about it. You don't *lose* anything by belonging to a committee to ban the bomb. Who's going to hurt you? Is the FBI going to stick you in jail?
>
> *Krassner*: There are certain employers who frown on it –

Presidential Papers was 'imperfect, incomplete, and somewhat deficient in its arithmetic. Its statistical studies are absent.' (p. 15) A piece of tactical humility which was diversionary, since the deficiencies of *The Presidential Papers* are not primarily statistical.

Mailer: Which employers? I think many good people are beginning to get a little complacent. The sort of good people who are militant and imaginative and active and brave and want a world they're willing to fight for; if there were a revolution they would carry a gun; if there were an underground they would fight a guerrilla war. But there is no real action for them and so they end up in what I think are essentially passive campaigns like 'Ban the Bomb'.[53]

In a sense Mailer was right about the ineffectual nature of the peace movement at that time – although he was perhaps wrong about the potential of these 'passive' protest movements generally. More importantly, he is of course writing about his own political predicament when he says that 'there is no real action for them'. His impatience and in fact his complacency are those of a *self-employed* writer cut off, as he put it in *Advertisements for Myself*, from 'an average man's experience . . . and what it was like to work at a dull job, or take orders from a man one hated.'[54] He is unable or unwilling to recognise that such activity in 1963 involves any risks and cuts short Krassner's suggestion that it does. The continual harassment of Peace Movement officials, the legislation existing in many American states against such demonstrations, and the intimidation and violence with which protest marches were met in the Southern states, is not considered. Later in the same interview he uses the phrase 'a gaggle of pacifists and vegetarians'[55] about Ban the Bomb supporters and derides their programme for being 'not manly'.[56] The stock, rhetorical hostility of this image indicates Mailer's total estrangement from the political movement he is describing; he can no longer see it with the tolerance of a liberal, let alone a critical socialist's attitude but deliberately chooses a Right-wing cliché. In comparison, his description of the student activists in *The Armies of the Night* on the eve of the Pentagon march shows a careful, detailed responsiveness which signals his reinvolvement in political activity. They are in a sense the very 'gaggle of pacifists and vegetarians' of five years before, and seen without the distancing cliché, they prove as 'manly' as Mailer himself.

The same year as *The Armies of the Night* (1968) Mailer published a short book on the Democratic and Republican Party

Conventions held in August 1968. In earlier books he had written memorable accounts of the Democratic Convention of 1960 which had nominated John F. Kennedy (*The Presidential Papers*) and of the Republican Convention of 1964 at which Barry Goldwater was nominated (*Cannibals and Christians*). In *Miami and the Siege of Chicago* Mailer again takes the Convention as a mirror of the American psyche, and his political reportage is in fact a frame for his old preoccupation with the state of America and his free-ranging apocalyptic prescriptions. His subject in these essays – the rituals of American political life – lends itself to Mailer's treatment rather better than did Cuba or Vietnam in *The Presidential Papers*. There is some excellent observation of the delegates and candidates, of American manners and social types, but little development in his political thinking.

In the essay on the Republican Convention in *Cannibals and Christians*, for example, Mailer analyses the nature of the support for Goldwater in America and shows considerable sensitivity to political trends of the period – in this case the emergence of the 'New Right' which crystallised around Goldwater's candidature:

> . . . southern delegates were firm as marble, firm as their hatred of Civil Rights. And there was much other strength for Barry from the Midwest and the West, a hard core of delegates filled with hot scalding hatred for the Eastern Establishment. . . . You could see them now with their Goldwater buttons, ensconced in every lobby, a Wasp Mafia where the grapes of wrath were stored. Not for nothing did the White Anglo-Saxon Protestant have a five-year subscription to *Reader's Digest* and *National Geographic*, high colonics and arthritis, silver-rimmed spectacles, punched-out bellies, and that air of controlled schizophrenia which is the merit badge for having spent one's life on Main Street.[57]

Yet whilst characterising the support for Goldwater in these terms, Mailer is able to admit his own excitement at the thought of Goldwater's victory. His reasons are partly political, resting on his own version of 'politique du pire'; Johnson will only blur the reality of America's conflicts whereas Goldwater will polarise America and out of that polarisation some hope for the revolution might come:

> For if Goldwater won . . . then at last a true underground
> might form; and liberty at the thought of any catalyst which
> could bring it on . . . Yes, the Goldwater movement excited
> the depths because the apocalypse was brought more
> near . . .[58]

But, as the above passage suggests, his socialist reasoning is
infused with a Marion Faye-type vision of the apocalypse, the
idea that national extinction would be better than survival
without radical change. Admitting that with Goldwater as
President the chances of a global nuclear war would be greater,
he nevertheless greets the possibility with excitement and, I
think, reveals the depths of his own political despair:

> And this had an appeal which burrowed deep, there was ex-
> citement at the thought of Goldwater getting the nomina-
> tion, as if now finally all one's personal suicides, all the
> deaths of the soul accumulated by the past, all the failures, all
> the terrors, could find purge in a national situation where
> national murder was being planned (the Third World War)
> and one's own suicide might be lost in a national suicide.
> There was that excitement that the burden of one's soul
> (always equal to the burden of one's personal responsibility)
> might finally be lifted – what a release was there![59]

The same strengths and weaknesses, and many of the same
political ambiguities of this essay, are present in *Miami and the
Siege of Chicago*: the acute observations coupled with the absurd
projection of his own vision on the events described. The
deeply-rooted radicalism is undercut by his impatience with orthodox Left-liberalism and the Black movements, but it is also
undercut by the equally deep-rooted conservatism and the
belief in 'the need to return to individual human effort'[60] which
he shares with the Wasp Republicans. There is however, a significant difference apparent in his treatment of the Chicago
Convention and the marches, demonstrations and battles
which took place there. At earlier Conventions, acting as a reporter, Mailer had observed the practice of American politics at
the top – the Presidential or Presidential candidate level. Political opposition – ideas about change or revolution – had been

interjections of his own, divorced from the reality of what was happening objectively. At Chicago, he found himself, like many other reporters, involved in a situation where large numbers of non-candidates and non-delegates had mobilised in an attempt to intervene politically in the issues of the Convention. Reporting this, often at second hand through the reports of other journalists, Mailer is able to identify with this movement or with sections of it. No longer a single and often eccentric voice commenting on the need for an 'underground', he sees himself in relation to others with similar objectives and finds that *a community of dissent already exists*. The passage which deals with this recognition is worth quoting in full; he addresses a meeting shortly after a confrontation between anti-Vietnam demonstrators and Daley's police force:

> So he had spoken at the bandshell. Standing there, seeing the crowd before him, feeling the predictable warmth of his power, all his courage was back, or so it felt – he was finally enough of an actor to face perils on a stage he would not meet as quickly other ways. And felt a surprising respect, even admiration, for the people on the benches and in the grass who had been tear-gassed day after day and were here now ready to march . . . Next, he went on to say that they were all at the beginning of a war which would continue for twenty years and this march today would be one battle in it. Then he explained that he would not be on this march because he had a deadline and could not take the chance, 'but you will all know what I am full of, if you don't see me on other marches' he had added, and they cheered him, cheered him enthusiastically even before he had said that he had come there merely to pay his respects and salute them. It affected him that they cheered him even for this relatively quietistic speech and when he was done, they cried out, 'Write it good, Baby,' and some young Negro from the Panthers or the Rangers or from where he did not know, serving as some kind of pro tem master of ceremonies now held his arm up high with his own. Black and white arms together in the air, he had been given a blessing by this Black . . .[61]

The language of this passage is that of a homecoming, as is signalled by the 'blessing' and the symbol of brotherhood, the

'black and white arms together'. As a political homecoming or
re-engagement, it is not simply the impulse of the moment; his
previous book *The Armies of the Night* documents the process
whereby Mailer reached this position and what reservations he
brought with him into the 'New Left'.

  The Armies of the Night describes a single political event, the
march on the Pentagon in October 1967 to protest against the
Vietnam war, and it locates this gesture of symbolic protest in a
history of American politics since the end of World War II. The
narrative is interrupted by Mailer's ruminations and reflections on liberal-technologues, women, students, Blacks, the
New Left, Leninists, and the hawk and dove argument about
the war in Vietnam. The chronological description of his involvement, from the initial reluctant agreement to participate
early in September to his arrival in Washington, the eve-of-
march session in the Ambassador Theatre, the early stages of
the march, Mailer's arrest, imprisonment, trial and release,
provides a framework within which the author-narrator discusses his own political history, assesses the current political
scene and comes to some sort of position with regard to it. He
had agreed to Mitch Goodman's request to attend with a mixture of misgivings and *auld lang syne* – 'memories of somewhat
more idealistic days in Paris'.[62] He had, as he points out, been
against the war in Vietnam from as early as 1965; in an essay in
Cannibals and Christians he had put forward an unconditional
demand that the US pull out of Vietnam, and had spoken in
Berkeley to the same effect that year. But he sees the demon-
stration as a distraction from his writing and poses his own
work in opposition to practical political involvement:

> One's own literary work was the only answer to the war in
> Vietnam.[63]

Once on the march, he reacts ambivalently; at times identifying
strongly with the participants, describing often with admiration the groups of students, and in particular, a Black student
militant who has chosen to protest against the war in Vietnam
rather than 'be out there somewhere agitating for Black
Power'.[64] He recognises the choices and risks involved for other
participants with a new awareness and sympathy. At other
moments, he is strongly tempted to leave, justifying his desire to

attend a party in New York that same evening, by dissociating himself if not from the politics of the marchers, from the march as a whole:

> Besides, he had no position here; it was not his March on the Pentagon in conception or execution.[65]

Scrupulously documenting these conflicting desires and loyalties, Mailer tells how he is reconciled to staying partly by the music of the Fugs and partly because he sees a role for himself – 'his function was to be arrested – his name was expendable for the cause'.[66]

One of the key reasons for this reconcilement is that the march although not his 'in conception or execution' comes closer to his own belief in 'open-ended' political activity than any organised by 'the bureaucrats of the Old Left'.[67] Involved in a mass political action, perhaps for the first time since the Wallace Campaign and the Progressive League in 1948, Mailer responds favourably to the spontaneity and anti-authoritarianism which he finds in the new movement. In his description of the New Left, Mailer clearly projects many of his own preoccupations and formulations on to the movement, but equally obviously, this movement actually offered him many reasons for doing so:

> this new generation of the Left hated the authority, because the authority lied. It lied through the teeth of corporation executives. and Cabinet officials and police enforcement officers and newspaper editors and advertising agencies and in its mass magazines . . . The New Left was drawing its political aesthetic from Cuba. The revolutionary idea which the followers of Castro had induced from their experience in the hills was that you created the revolution first and learned from it, learned of what your revolution might consist and where it might go . . .[68]

Mailer sees the alienation of this new generation from the authority of the American state as similar in many ways to his own, as the above passage adequately illustrates. He can make common cause with them, as he couldn't with the 'bureaucrats of the Old LEFT', whose adherence to 'the solid-as-brick-work-logic-of the-next-step'[69] he identifies with the forces of totalitarianism and the bureaucrats of the American capitalist state. This analysis of the New Left's alienation, together with the open-ended nature of their strategy and tactics, gives Mailer enough space to fit himself and his political and philosophical preoccupations of the last twenty years.

Later in the Occoquan jail, Mailer's comments on Teague, a Leninist of the old type, confirm this view. Listening to Teague's analysis of the march, Mailer mentally rebuts the Marxist-Leninist position and methods which Teague exemplifies:

> Everything Teague said was probably true, and yet the indictment was too easy – it had all the firm hard impact of all the sound-as-brickwork-logic-of-the-next-step – he had heard Communists and Trotskyists expatiating on social problems and social actions for years with just this same militant, precise, executive command in analysing the situation, the same compelling sense of structure, same satisfying almost happy dissection and mastication of the bones and tendons of the problem before them, and Mailer had in fact decided years ago, repelled by some bright implacable certainty in the voices of such full-time Marxists, that Leninism finally was good for Leninists about the way psychoanalysis was good for psychoanalysts ... Leninism was built to analyse a world in which all the structures were made of steel – now the sinews of society were founded on transistors so small Dragon Lady could hide them beneath her nail.[70]

With this statement, Mailer gives his own bearings; he has moved from the straight class politics (Marxism–Leninism) of the late forties, through a period of disengagement and mysticised existentialism in the fifties, to a new politics of consciousness in the American New Left. He can find common ground politically with Black and student elements (his work has found a receptive audience among these sections) but, as the comments on women and his wives in *The Armies of the Night* suggest, he is unable to relate to the other key element in the new politics – the ideas of the emerging women's liberation movement. His book, *The Prisoner of Sex*, published three years later, was to deal with just this problem. He has not, clearly, realised his hope of making 'a revolution in the consciousness of our time' and in *Miami and the Siege of Chicago* he takes stock of this fact with some personal bitterness. Having for years fought the battle, as he conceived it, on his own, he recognises in the late sixties that there is an existing army ('armies') on the American political scene and that his problem is now whether he can afford the price of re-enlistment:

Where was his true engagement? To be forty-five years old, and have lost a sense of where his loyalties belonged – to the revolution or to the stability of the country (at some painful personal price it could be perceived) was to bring on himself the anguish of the European intellectual in the Thirties. And the most powerful irony for himself is that he had lived for a dozen empty hopeless years after the Second World War with the bitterness, rage and potential militancy of a real revolutionary, he had had some influence perhaps on this generation of Yippies now in the street, but no revolution had arisen in the years when he was ready – the timing of his soul was apocalyptically maladroit.[71]

The political perspectives of *A Fire on the Moon* and *The Prisoner of Sex* suggest that Mailer does not envisage a revolution which would meet his conditions, for which he would be 'ready'. Although he still writes of himself as a revolutionary, a combatant in the political struggle against the totalitarian state, he is even less sanguine about the nature of revolutionary possibilities and about his role within such a struggle. In *The Prisoner of Sex* he no longer imagines himself as a 'general' but appears simply as 'the man' facing communards who are largely hostile to his ideas about the future. While defending his revolutionary credentials, Mailer appears in this last book to suspect that the New Left (and especially the women's contingent) has betrayed the cause and that his own loyalties may belong to the radicalism of the past:

. . . he knew that no matter how conservative he became, nor how much he began to believe that the marrows and sinews of creation were locked in the roots of the amputated past, he was still a revolutionary, for conservatism had been destroyed by the corporations of the conservatives, their plastic, their advertising, their technology.[72]

3 'The Best Writer in America'

BEGINNINGS

Mailer started writing whilst still at Harvard under the influence of various thirties' writers – principally Farrell, Dos Passos and Steinbeck. The stories from this period, some of which are reprinted in *Advertisements for Myself*, show this influence very clearly. One of the best of these, written in 1943 (a year before Mailer went into the American army), is an attempt to write about war, and it forms an interesting contrast to *The Naked and the Dead*. In 'A Calculus at Heaven', the remnants of an American company are isolated in a house on the edge of a swamp shortly before a Japanese attack in which they are all killed. The characters represent a cross-section of American types: a priest from a poor Irish family, a captain who was a Boston painter in an unhappy marriage before being drafted, a courageous and brutalised Italian, a blond football-playing Jew, and an Indian sergeant. There is an omniscient viewpoint of the action with flashbacks to the civilian life of the soldiers, and the alienation of the individual men from the army and the war emerges as one of the main themes. Thus, although the narrative technique and situation is different from that of *The Naked and the Dead*, some of the same themes and literary devices are already present in this early short story.

It was influenced, Mailer says in *Advertisements for Myself*[1], by Malraux's *Man's Fate*, but the American influences seem to predominate. The civilian flashbacks are a pastiche of Dos Passos' and the writing about combat, which is brisk and effective, is strongly reminiscent of Hemingway. The style, particularly where the author attempts to deal with certain philosophical issues, is often crude and recalls the worst elements of

76

Steinbeck's prose:

> He wanted suddenly to know why the hell he was gonna get his. He just wanted to know what it was all about. They called him Creepy Joe around the army camps, and said he knew all the answers 'cause he never asked questions. But he had to ask questions now, because he was buying something that cost a lot. He'd never asked what fightin' was about; fightin' was his business, and you didn't ask questions if business was good, but now he kinda like to know.[2]

This attempt to evoke the pathos of the inarticulate man faced with death and to convey the alienation of the professional soldier from the issues of the war, is effectively ruined by the repetitious and sententious language. Although there are moments of comparable crudeness in *The Naked and the Dead* (as with the death of Roth for example) these appear as minor flaws in the full-length novel. The patrol is much more flexible and richer in possibilities as a narrative situation than the besieged town in 'A Calculus at Heaven'; the ideological concerns have been shifted and dramatised into the Cummings –Hearn dialogues, the prose is generally tighter and there is a much more developed use of image and symbol.

The influence of Dos Passos and Farrell is still paramount however; the generalisations and social criticisms in *The Naked and the Dead* are made through concrete descriptions and careful dialogue and the interchapter biographies combine the techniques of the biographies and narrative sections of *USA*. The debt is not merely a technical one, since many of the ideas are clearly continuous with the social vision at the base of Dos Passos' trilogy. The deterministic attitude towards character which emerges from the ten 'Time Machine' sections is to some extent a legacy from the naturalism of the thirties which Mailer seems to have assumed along with the experimental use of biography and the newsreel style of the social commentary. The sexual determinism – the oversimplification of motivation and behaviour in terms of sex – is most evident with Croft and Cummings though it is present in the other characterisations. Cummings' sexual ambiguities are presented as the product of an over-authoritarian father and an indulgent hyper-feminine mother; as an adult his coldness in heterosexual relations forces his wife into infidelity while he sublimates his sexual energies into advancing his military career. Thus his search for power is presented in terms of his suppressed homosexuality, and this psychological explanation is not fully integrated with his political role within the novel. The suggestion, for example, that he is sexually attracted to Hearn and that this sexual desire is what lies behind his desire to dominate him, over-determines the presentation of the relationship. The desire to dominate a difficult junior officer is already sufficiently explained by Cummings' political views on the 'fear-ladder' structure of the army. Whilst Mailer's general point about the inter-connections between sexuality and the psychology of fascism works very well in *The Naked and the Dead*, his characterisations are marred at specific places by an over-insistence on this point.

Despite the schematic conception and sometimes crude presentation, Mailer's characterisations show much detailed and subtle observation of individual motives, and each of his numerous characters is distinct from the others. In the context of the narrative as a whole, they are successful, realistic characterisations, and with Gallagher and Valsen, for example, Mailer manages with some skill to integrate the psychological and sociological factors which have molded their characters. In the 'Time Machine', entitled 'The Wandering Minstrel', using the historic present, Mailer describes Valsen's childhood in a small mining town in Montana. The description moves between Red's specific history in this situation and an overall view of the experience of a poor mining community:

> By the time he is fourteen he is able to use a drill. Good money for a kid, but down in the shafts, at the extreme end of the tunnel, there isn't room to stand. Even a kid works in a crouch, his feet stumbling in the refuse of the ore that has been left from filling the last cart. It's hot of course, and damp, and the lights from their helmets are lost quickly in the black corridors. The drill is extremely heavy and a boy has to hold the butt against his chest . . .[3]

'He' at the start of this passage refers explicitly to the fourteen year old Valsen, but by the end of the paragraph the same pronoun refers to '*a* kid', '*a* boy', that is, any boy who is forced to work in the mines at his age. This device is a key one in *The*

Naked and the Dead, it is used to suggest the social as well as the individual nature of character formation, and to make clear in this case that Red is one of the many – is a representative of a type. (The generalisations about his 'case' are supported by a great deal of detail and in particular an excellent vignette of a dishwasher's life.) In order to escape the life of a miner, the physical hardship, frequent accidents, periods of unemployment which had shaped his father's life, Valsen deserts his mother and family, and this choice, in its turn, shapes his life. The pattern is confirmed when he abandons the woman and child with whom he has lived fairly happily for several years in pursuit of a 'freedom' which turns out to be a 'hobo jungle',[4] ill-health and a resentful boredom. Mailer suggests his natural intelligence, his capacity for warmth and affection, have been blunted and distorted by the conditions in which he finds himself, and the portrait is a convincing one. What has been suggested in the 'Time Machine' is dramatised in the narrative where his fear of commitment to the men in the platoon impoverishes his experience and undermines his potential leadership. Biography and narrative converge and the plausibility of his symbolic defeat by Croft rests on both.

The characters in *The Naked and the Dead* were carefully researched, as Mailer's *Paris Review* interview reveals.[5] He kept a long *dossier* on each man, with many details which were not used in the novel, had charts to show which characters had not yet had scenes with others, and used his sociological data methodically and, I think, to good effect in the novel. In the same interview Mailer comments critically on this method of writing and its effects on the structure of *The Naked and the Dead*:

> For a book which seems spontaneous on its surface, *The Naked and the Dead* was written mechanically. I studied engineering at Harvard, and I suppose it was the work of a young engineer. The structure is sturdy, but there's no fine filigree to the joints. Just spot-welding and riveting. And the working plan was very simple. I devised some preliminary actions for the platoon in order to give the reader an opportunity to get to know the men, but this beginning as I said, took over two thirds of the book. The patrol itself is also simple, but I did give more thought to working it out ahead of time.[6]

Though 'very simple' and undoubtedly derivative, the structure of *The Naked and the Dead* is one of its greatest strengths. In no other novel, except perhaps in *An American Dream*, has Mailer produced the same structural coherence and unity of design. *The Naked and the Dead* is a novel of ideas based firmly in the realistic tradition – unlike *An American Dream*, which uses another novelistic convention to provide a unifying framework. The former describes, in four parts, a successful attempt to capture a small south Pacific island from the Japanese in World War II; it provides a detailed and realistic account of an I & R platoon, from their initial landing, in combat, through a reconnaissance patrol, to the conclusion and aftermath of the battle. Intercut with this narrative, are the interchapter biographies, and the scenes in which the General conducting the campaign is presented. Thus a comprehensive yet minutely particularised account is given of the progress of the campaign. The juxtaposition of the fragmented physical experience of the enlisted men with Cummings' highly structured overall conception of the war, is itself one of the themes of the novel – the undemocratic nature of an army involved in fighting against fascism. The form serves the ideological concerns and although certain realistic conventions are used, the novel is in no sense 'naturalistic' in terms of its fictional organisation. As Mailer says, the number of events experienced by the platoon could not possibly have happened to any one army platoon. Similarly the two parties into which the platoon splits at the close of the novel serve a symbolic function which is barely consistent with the realistic possibilities of the situation. *The Naked and the Dead*, as Mailer emphasised,

> is not a realistic documentary; it is rather a 'symbolic' book of which the basic theme is the conflict between the beast and the seer in man.[7]

In fact, it is the tightly-organised 'sturdy' structure and the realistic detail which hold the symbolic elements in check. The theme of the beast and the seer (discussed in the chapter on Mailer's heroes) is treated mainly through the patterns of animal imagery and the use of Mount Anaka. Where the descriptions of combat (and the movement of the machine guns and Martinez's scouting expedition) offer what Hemingway called the 'sequence of fact and motion which made the emotion', Mount Anaka is Mailer's 'constitutive' symbol:

> The mountain the platoon attempts to climb represents death and man's creative urge, fate, and man's desire to conquer the elements – all kinds of things you never dream of separating and stating so baldly.[8]

The mountain dominates the island physically and looms over the consciousness of each of the characters. For Croft and Cummings it symbolises power and their efforts to achieve power in their own lives; their political and emotional kinship is symbolised in their identification with it. The others' more ambiguous attitudes suggest, in different degrees, their hopes and fears about their lives and the fact of death. The passage in which Croft's reaction to Mount Anarka is described shows something of the strain which this over-large symbol imposed on Mailer's prose style:

> Croft was moved as deeply, as fundamentally as caissons resettling in the river mud. The mountain attracted him, taunted and inflamed with its size. He had never seen it so clearly before. Mired in the jungle, the cliffs of Watamai Range had obscured the mountain. He stared at it now, examined its ridges, feeling an instinctive desire to climb the mountain and stand on its peak, to know that all that mighty weight was beneath his feet. His emotions were intense; he knew awe and hunger and the peculiar ecstasy he had felt after Henessey was dead, or when he killed the Japanese prisoner.[9]

In contrast to the overblown style of these 'symbolic' passages, there is the Hemingwayesque simplicity of the description of Croft in action:

> 'Shit.' Croft's hand found the flare-box, and he loaded the gun again. He was beginning to see in the darkness, and he hesitated. But something moved on the river and he fired the flare. As it burst, a few Japanese soldiers were caught motionless in the water. Croft pivoted his gun on them and fired. One of the soldiers remained standing for an incredible time. There was no expression on his face; he looked vacant

and surprised even as the bullets struck him in the chest.[10]

In *The Naked and the Dead* Mailer encompasses an incredible variety of prose styles, tones and voices borrowed from a multitude of other writers, but does not, I think, create a distinctive voice of his own. When in *Barbary Shore* he abandoned the omniscient voice and the techniques borrowed from the thirties novelists, it was to create a structurally confused allegory with an indistinct first-person narrator. Lovett, the 'I' who is a writer with a lost memory, is the spokesman for the writer who had rejected the borrowed composite voice of his first novel and not yet found an alternative.

Abandoning the social vision of the thirties, Mailer also abandoned realistic characterisation, tight narrative structure and an omniscient authorial voice. The decision to attempt something new, stylistically, is announced in the very first line of *Barbary Shore*. 'Probably I was in the war'[11] is a very different tone and association from anything in *The Naked and the Dead* or in the short stories written at Harvard. The uncertainty which introduces the fact of Lovett's amnesia is also a built-in feature of the novel. What he attempted in *Barbary Shore* owes much to the European novel of atmosphere (specifically Kafka and Dostoevsky), a lot to Nathanael West's neo-surrealist black comedy, and something to Faulkner:

> I had read *The Sound and the Fury* a month or two earlier and it had a long influence on me. Its first undigested force is obvious in 'Maybe Next Year', but the style, or should we say, the borrowing, appears again in *Barbary Shore* with McLeod's soliloquy to Lovett, and it is done best perhaps with Elena's letter in *The Deer Park*.[12]

The allegory set forth depends mainly on the sheer pressure of the rhetorical language and on images and symbols used as unifying motifs. Mailer was, I think, trying to write about the Revolution and its effects on the present as Faulkner wrote about the Southern past and its hold on the Southern mind.

The characters exist as personified ideas, without any of the sociological or psychological detail of the characters of *The Naked and the Dead*. Although there is some important development, psychologically, of the relationship between Hollingsworth and McLeod as interrogator and his victim, the characters and their relation to each other are alive only in terms of the allegory. The purest example of this method is Lannie Madison – her name itself suggests her allegorical function. Her madness is intended to symbolise the alienation and confusion of the modern political consciousness after the betrayal of the Russian Revolution. She and Lovett (whose amnesia is the symbol of his alienation) represent the split halves of the modern Left, and their sterile love-making underlines that splitting. Her speech, full of allusions and quotations from *King Lear*, Keats, Sherwood Anderson and Trotsky, and her 'abnormal' sexuality, are the ways in which Mailer tries to symbolise her political estrangement in the dislocation of her personality. But because these symbols are inadequate (her walking through the streets of Brooklyn in pyjamas, for example, appears rather more like zaniness than schizophrenia), the attempt is pathetic. She is chiefly memorable as the mouthpiece of the image of 'L'univers concentrationaire' – the coherence of which is not entirely compatible with her other statements. One of the chief problems is that this image of poetic despair is not integrated with the comic, neo-surrealist elements which centre around Guinivere and Monina. The scenes with Lannie and Guinivere together show this particularly clearly. Guinivere, although no more 'realistically' presented, is a far more effective symbolic creation. Treated in an absurdist manner reminiscent of Faye Doyle in Nathanael West's *Miss Lonelyhearts*, she serves as a real indictment of American womanhood corrupted by mass entertainment – shallow, confused and obsessed by her own pseudo-sexuality.

The structural incoherence of the novel, particularly in its ending, expresses Mailer's intellectual confusions of that period. Besides the political ideas which were being worked out within the novel ('I started *Barbary Shore* as some sort of a fellow traveller and finished with a political position which was a far-flung mutation of Trotskyism'[13]) there were a number of new ideas for which he was not yet able to find any imaginative embodiment:

Barbary Shore was built on the division which existed then in

> my mind. My conscious intelligence, as I've indicated,
> became obsessed by the Russian Revolution. But my
> unconscious was much more interested in other matters:
> murder, suicide, orgy, psychosis, all the themes I discuss in
> *Advertisements for Myself*. Since the gulf between these con-
> scious and unconscious themes was vast and quite resistant
> to any quick literary coupling, the tension to get a bridge
> across resulted in the peculiar feverish hothouse atmosphere
> of the book. My unconscious felt one kind of dread, my con-
> scious mind another, and *Barbary Shore* lives somewhere be-
> tween . . . It was a book written without any plan.[14]

In fact Mailer uses Lovett's amnesia not merely as a political
symbol but to provide, at least for the first eight chapters, the
novel's framework. The first-person narrative of the would-be
writer's sojourn in a Brooklyn boarding-house is interrupted by
images/fantasies from his unknown past. Whereas the in-
terchapters in *The Naked and the Dead* offer information and
explanation in support of the line of narrative, Lovett's fantasy
memories serve rather a different function. First they introduce
most of the major themes and, secondly, through the repetition
of certain refrains and images, they serve as a unifying force in
the novel. The first use is Mailer's attempt to concretise certain
abstractions; but although he sometimes achieves some interesting, highly suggestive effects (as with Lovett's fantasies of the
battles of the Cossacks) many of the images are not powerful
enough to do this effectively and seem obstructive and con-
trived. One of these occurs in the opening chapter, where the
narrator sees a man returning home in a taxi, unable to recognise his surroundings:

> The man lives in this city, but he has never seen these streets.
> The architecture is strange, and the people are dressed in un-
> familiar clothing. He looks at a sign, but it is printed in an
> alphabet he cannot read.[15]

The image is clearly intended to suggest the estrangement and
dispossession that characterise the narrator and, by implication, many of his generation. But the image is no more resonant than an explicit statement containing the words
'estrangement' or 'alienation'. Similarly the 'little object'

which is used as a symbol for what is missing in the different characters' lives is, I think, insufficiently concretised; stolen by McLeod, sought by the FBI agent and eventually inherited by Lovett, it seems to symbolise some kind of hope, vision or wisdom. Its symbolic value rests on the fact that it is sought after, not on the mystery of what it is, but by refusing to invest its symbolic qualities in any concrete object (as say, in a set of papers) and by calling it always 'the little object', Mailer only draws attention unnecessarily to the fact that it is a *symbol*. The use of the refrain 'So the blind will lead the blind, and the deaf shout warnings to one another until their voices are lost' at the beginning and end of the novel (and at several points during the narrative) as a unifying device does not succeed in holding together many warring elements in the book, which as Mailer commented in *Advertisements for Myself*, 'collapsed into a chapter of political speech and never quite recovered'.[16] McLeod's speech ceases to belong to McLeod very early in that chapter and at this point the characters and fictional situation drop away, leaving only the author struggling with his own political and intellectual preoccupations. The novel is brought to a hasty end with the narrative element formally dealt with (McLeod's suicide, Lannie's arrest, Hollingsworth and Guinivere's departure for Barbary and Lovett's escape) but with no real resolution of the novel's actual substance.

His third novel, *The Deer Park*, represents another attempt to make a 'bridge' between the concerns of his 'conscious intelligence' and the themes which were to occupy a central position in his middle and later works: 'murder, suicide, orgy, psychosis'. The mixture of styles reflects this division and the tension between these interests. Desert D'Or and Eitel and Elena's relationship are treated for the most part fairly traditionally, and in this sense *The Deer Park* shows a return to some of the fictional techniques Mailer had jettisoned in *Barbary Shore*. There is the same psychological realism in the treatment of character and a similar use of concrete detail and dialogue that one finds in *The Naked and the Dead*. In these respects *The Deer Park* is a logical development, both stylistically and thematically, from his first novel. The scenes dealing with Faye and Sergius, on the other hand, have a much greater resemblance to sections of *Barbary Shore*. The extended sentence structures, the special kind of rhetorical language which were used to convey Lovett's fantasies, the images of Barbary and the concentration-camp future, are used to describe Sergius' view of 'time as the connection of new circuits'[17] and Faye's apocalyptic vision of destruction:

> So let it come, Faye thought, let this explosion come, and then another, and all the others, until the Sun God burned the earth. Let it come, the thought, looking into the east at Mecca where the bombs ticked while he stood on a tiny rise of ground trying to see one hundred, two hundred, three hundred miles across the desert. Let it come Faye begged, like a man praying for rain, let it come and clear away the rot and the stench and the stink, let it come for all of everywhere, just so it comes and the world stands clear in the white dead dawn.[18]

The narrative fails to integrate these disparate elements and as with *Barbary Shore* the novel falters about three quarters of the way through. Nevertheless Mailer makes considerable advances with his new long sentence – his attempt to contain the contradictions, nuances, the urgencies and qualifications of his vision of the world. In his portrait of Eitel's moral dissolution too, Mailer conveys with great realism and economy the interrelationship between his failure as an artist and as a man. The process by which he reduces the possibilities of the relationship to the technical problems of an affair is enacted in the language and his moral and intellectual decline is mirrored in the clichés in which, increasingly, he allows himself to think:

> The inevitable progress of a love-affair, Eitel thought. One began with the notion that life had found its flavour, and ended with the familiar distaste of no adventure and no novelty. It was one of the paradoxes he had cherished. The unspoken purpose of freedom was to find love, yet when love was found one could only desire freedom again.[19]

In this passage Eitel is 'placed' very precisely and astutely as a man who 'cherishes' convenient paradoxes, who accepts 'inevitability' as sufficient explanation for his actions. This example is one of the ways in which the abstract statement that 'Life had made (Eitel) a determinist'[20] is concretely illustrated. In sections of *The Deer Park* Mailer shows the same kind of psychological insight and stylistic control that he achieved in the best parts of *The Naked and the Dead*. The sections concerned with Eitel generally have an internal coherence and realism with which Faye's apocalyptic interjections fail to connect. Sergius, in his role as Eitel's disciple and Lulu's lover, works well enough but as he becomes another 'existential' hero, Mailer is forced to construct a world outside the bounds of realistic time and space where he can communicate with Eitel 'in the passing fire of his imagination'.[21]

To some extent the flaws of *The Deer Park* may be attributed to the publication and revision problems which he discusses at length in *Advertisements for Myself*. It was the novel, he says, in which he felt that he was finally sloughing off the literary influences on which he had depended in his first two novels. Whilst revising the first draft of *The Deer Park*,

> the style of the work lost its polish, became rough, and I can say real, because there was an abrupt and muscular body back of the voice now. It had been there all the time, trapped in the porcelain of a false style, but now I chipped away . . . I felt as if I was finally learning how to write.[22]

This process is discernible in the complicated narrative procedure and in the changes that take place in the narrative voice. The novel begins in the first person, as O'Shaughnessy presents a prolonged introduction of himself, the setting and characters. Only in Part II does the story begin. Again O'Shaughnessy is the narrating voice although he participates less. In the third part the narrator's role in the action decreases still further – ('I have the conceit I *know* what happened').[23] Here he is referring to the Eitel–Elena affair which is told in the third person, although O'Shaughnessy's tone colours the presentation. In effect the point of view becomes that of a first person observer with omniscient powers, except during his affair with Lulu Meyers which is dramatised in the first person throughout. Later O'Shaughnessy relies on secondary sources for information and after his departure from Desert D'Or, on letters and hearsay – ('I heard from a waitress what had happened to Marion and Elena')[24]. After settling in New York, the narrator becomes a sort of visionary observer transcending the bounds of time and space to converse with an unseen Eitel and an imagined God. This method reveals, I think, Mailer's uncertainties about the relative importance of his three main protagonists, and it points to his problems with voice. The uneveness of O'Shaughnessy's tone and voice (he sounds at times close to Nick Carraway in *The Great Gatsby* and at other times close to Mailer's own voice in *The Armies of the Night*) also represents Mailer's attempt to free himself from the 'porcelain of a false style' and to discover a more 'muscular' voice with which to express his new 'existential' ideas.

NEW BEGINNINGS

In his fourth book, *Advertisements for Myself* (published in 1959), Mailer finds the 'muscular' voice which had been nascent in *Barbary Shore* and sections of *The Deer Park*, but significantly in doing so he moves outside the novel form. The problems of the writer were touched on in both his second and third novels; both have narrators who are writers trying to write novels. At the beginning of *Barbary Shore*, in conversation with the playwright Willie Dinsmore, Lovett rejects the literary dogmatism and thirties-influenced conception of art as 'a people's fight'.[25] For him, Dinsmore's simplistic literary principles are useless weapons against the complexities of the new totalitarianism. In *The Deer Park*, describing the struggle between commercialism and creativity of yet another artist, O'Shaughnessy rejects both commercialism and the example of other writers:

> because finally the crystallisation of their experience did not have a texture apposite to my experience.[26]

He gives up the novel about bull fighters (because Hemingway had already covered that ground) to try to write *The Deer Park*, sustained by 'the intolerable conviction that I could write about worlds I knew better than anyone else alive'.[27] At the beginning of *Advertisements for Myself*, another first-person narrator-writer, Mailer himself, describes *his* conviction:

> that my present and future work will have the deepest influence of any work being done by an American novelist in these years.[28]

Thus although *Advertisements for Myself* represents a rupture in terms of style and form with all that Mailer had previously attempted, there are also certain important continuities.

The collection of stories, essays and journalism which make up *Advertisements for Myself* is perhaps best approached from this standpoint. In effect, between and beyond the individual pieces, is the story of Norman Mailer the writer – his problems, humiliations and achievements. The decision to use his 'personality as the armature of the book'[29] provides the unifying framework and it makes it radically different from an ordinary anthology. The stories and essays are not intended or permitted to stand by themselves but are an integral part of the larger narrative. In the 'advertisements' which preface the individual pieces, Mailer repeatedly makes the point that literature in America is a commodity which is bought, sold and advertised, and his title *Advertisements for Myself*, amongst other things, draws attention to this fact. In the 'Fourth Advertisement' subtitled 'The Last Draft of Deer Park' which dominates Part III of the book, he describes how this recognition was forced on him and with what effect. His innocent assumptions about the relations between writers and publishers were destroyed by the legal and personal battles with Rinehart to publish *The Deer Park* and by his subsequent struggle to find an alternative publisher:

> I realised in some bottom of myself that for years I had been the sort of comic figure I would have cooked to a turn in one of my books, a radical who had the nineteenth-century naivete to believe that the people with whom he did business were 1) gentlemen, 2) fond of him and 3) respectful of his ideas even if in disagreement with them.[30]

Despite the somewhat maudlin irony of this statement, Mailer's real bitterness at the experience emerges. It shattered his idealistic conception of the writer's role and confronted him with the fact – apparently for the first time – that there are market demands as well as aesthetic problems facing the modern writer:

> And so as the language of sentiment would have it, something broke in me, but I do not know if it was so much a loving heart, as a cyst on the weak, the unreal, and the needy and I

was finally open to my anger. I turned within my psyche I can almost believe, for I felt something shift to murder in me. I finally had the simple sense to understand that if I wanted my work to travel further than others, the life of my talent depended on fighting a little more and looking for help a little less.[31]

The violence of this reaction centred on the fact that, having from his Harvard days built his identity on the idea of being a 'writer', the experience of literary failure and rejection constituted a real crisis of identity for him. The impact of the experience was heightened by the enormous success of his first novel, while the hostility which had greeted his second novel, *Barbary Shore*, made the publication and reception of the third, *The Deer Park*, a critical point in his career as a writer.

The title and form of *Advertisements for Myself* are governed by this new sense of himself as a writer in a market situation. His competitiveness with other writers, in 'Quick and Expensive Comments on the Talent in the Room', is a part of this; he is advertising for an audience and competing, as it were, with all the rival products on the market. Just how far he had changed can be seen from a statement he made in 1948, shortly after the publication of *The Naked and the Dead*:

I think it is much better when people who read your books don't know anything about you, even what you look like. I have refused to let *Life* photograph me. Getting your mug in the papers is one of the shameful ways of making a living.[32]

He has moved from seeing writing as a 'vocation' to the conception of it as a career, to be 'greased'[33] by a PR man or himself. Far from finding it 'shameful' any longer, Mailer consciously exploits his personality. The 'advertisements' discuss the author's intentions and criticisms of the stories they precede, destroying the impersonality of the author and inviting identification between reader and writer. One of the best examples of this is in the 'Advertisement for *Barbary Shore*' where he discusses his problems of what to write after *The Naked and the Dead*:

If my past had become empty as a theme, was I to write about Brooklyn streets, or my mother and father, or another war

novel (*The Naked and the Dead go to Japan*) was I to do the book
of the returning veteran when I had lived like a mole writing
and rewriting seven hundred pages in those fifteen months?[34]

Mailer is here writing about the writer's problem of using his
recent past as fictional material, when that past had in fact been
spent writing a novel! There is a degree of humorous self-
consciousness here which completely undermines the traditional writer-reader relationship and directly prefigures his
later experiments – particularly *The Armies of the Night*.

In one of the longest pieces in *Advertisements for Myself*, 'The
Man who Studied Yoga', Mailer gives the novelist's problems a
fictional treatment. The relationship of Sam Slovoda, ex-
radical and novelist *manqué*, and his wife Eleanor is presented
realistically, and the dialogue between them and their New
York friends is based on acute observation of the mores and
intonations of the liberal academic social group. The nuances
of their relationship, 'that pomade of affection, resentment,
boredom and occasional compassion',[35] are conveyed with an
excellent balance of irony and sympathy but certain elements
in the story, like the presence of the omniscient anonymous narrator for example, are not fully integrated with this level. Originally 'The Man who Studied Yoga' was conceived as the
prologue to a long ambitious novel, or series of novels, which
were abandoned for *Advertisements for Myself*. The reasons are
suggested in the novella itself when Sam Slovoda is asked by
one of his friends if he has given up his projected novel:

> Sam says, 'Temporarily.' He cannot find a form, he explains.
> He does not want to write a realistic novel, because reality is
> no longer realistic.[36]

'Reality', he implies, lies outside the scope of realistic treatment. Mailer, despite his considerable abilities to portray
character, relationships and emotional states of great complexity (as evidenced in both *The Deer Park* and 'The Man Who
Studied Yoga') shows in *Advertisements for Myself* an increasing
reluctance to write realistically about such subjects. This is, I
think, partly a consequence of his desire to 'make a revolution
in the consciousness of our time'. If he had continued to write
realistically about characters like Slovoda, he would have been

forced to write about what seemed to him to be capitulation, to become himself a 'chronicler of defeat'. At the end of 'The Man Who Studied Yoga' the narrator leaves Sam to his life of 'dreary compromise',[37] and this can be taken in some sense as Mailer's own decision.

With 'The White Negro', 'The Time of Her Time', and 'Advertisements for Myself on the Way Out', Mailer makes it out of the 'porcelain' of other writers' styles, moves away from the passive, doomed heroes like Eitel and Slovoda, and away from the realistic technique which he felt would lead him into literary despair and possibly silence. The move from description to imaginative prescription is obvious in 'The White Negro'; the white Negro, or the American existentialist is clearly a fictional creation, a hero with the courage of Croft and the philosophical outlook of Sergius and Faye, released from the confines of a realistic fictional structure. Ned Polsky in his criticism of the essay reprinted in *Advertisements for Myself* calls the hipster 'the gorgeous flower of Mailer's romantic idealism',[38] and this seems to me an accurate description. He is based on a minority of urban, jazz-oriented black Negroes, who are marginal to Black and White cultures in America, but he exists only in the world of Mailer's fictional imagination. Mailer himself confounded the issue, I think, by defending himself from what were essentially sociological criticisms. Whilst arguments can be raised about the relation of Mailer's 'hipster' to certain groups then in America, the essay itself stands or falls finally not on its empirical objectivity but as an imaginative construct.

In his introduction of the hipster, the American existentialist, Mailer had this to say about his situation and response:

> if our collective condition is to live with instant death by atomic war, relatively quick death by the State as *l'univers concentrationnaire*, or with a slow death by conformity with every creative and rebellious instinct stifled (at what damage to the mind and the heart and the liver and the nerves no research foundation for cancer will discover in a hurry), if the fate of twentieth-century man is to live with death from adolescence to premature senescence, why then the only life-giving answer is to accept the terms of death, to live with death as immediate danger, to divorce oneself from

society, to exist without roots, to set out on that uncharted journey into the rebellious imperatives of the self.[39]

This proposition contains many of the ideas and contradictions of the twenty-page essay. Its demands – 'to accept the terms of death, to live with death' – come close to Marion Faye's vision of annihilation, but the essay also embodies Sergius' 'glimmer of the joy of the flesh' in its celebration of the orgasm. Mailer defines the hipster's situation in a life-and-death metaphor which is only half metaphorical, since 'instant death by atomic war' may have seemed a real enough possibility in 1957 when the essay was originally written. The 'slow death by conformity' is further qualified as a state where every 'creative and rebellious instinct (is) stifled'. The positives of the essay are introduced here; the linkage of 'creative' and 'rebellious' is fundamental to the ideas of the piece. Behind this early coupling lies the assumption that American life at all levels works against creativity, and that to be creative one must therefore *rebel* against all the norms of that culture.

The long sentence with its rhetorical structure ('if our collective condition is to live . . . why then the only life-giving answer is . . . to live') is typical of the prose of the whole essay: highly rhetorical, carefully structured and with all its metaphors closely integrated. The parenthesis develops the life-and-death image by referring to the 'damage' incurred in the course of 'slow death by conformity' and introduces another key term in the diagnosis of American life – cancer. But after the brisk statement of the three kinds of death, the parenthesis with its deliberative repetitions ('to the mind and the heart and the liver and the nerves') also serves to slow the rhetorical pace, before the acceleration of the last lines. The repetitions in the last half of the sentence with its five infinitives ('to accept . . . to live . . . to divorce . . . to exist . . . to set out') heighten the rhythmic qualities, gather momentum and give the last line the maximum force and finality.

In both 'The Time of Her Time' and 'Way Out' Mailer uses this new 'muscular' prose in which he is able to express the urgencies and ironies of his new vision. From the early fidelity to everyday speech rhythms and a reliance on visual imagery, he moves to a synthesis of sound and image and the repetition of individual words and phrases with a new emphasis on tactile and olfactory imagery. Another new stylistic development in 'Way Out' is the sudden, seemingly gratuitous concretisation of detail, such as that about Faye's microscope:

> the valve of a snail shell as seen through his microscope (Zeiss 2,000 Deutschmarks, oil immersion, binocular eyepiece) was a spiral galaxy of horny cells whose pigmentation had the deep orange of a twilight sun.[40]

The parenthetic information does add something to the characterisation of Faye – that he indulges and can afford to indulge his whims with some of the most expensive equipment – but it draws attention to the microscope far beyond any need imposed by the plot or characterisation. It may be seen as an ironic bow to the ubiquity of advertising in modern life and as such is a continuation of the theme announced in his title; but more than this, it is a parody of popular fiction techniques in the form of an aside from the author to the reader, which effectively forces the reader down from any merely 'aesthetic' involvement with the text of the story. This new stylistic self-consciousness is present in the narrator's commentary. The narrator is a again a writer, and one who discusses the felicity of his metaphors and current theorists of the novel within the story:

> Now I know it is not the mode of our pompous obliteration-haunted years to encourage such pathetic fallacies as the animism of the wind and an old house, but since (be I ghost, *geist*, demi-urge, dog, bud, flower, tree, house or some lost way-station of the divine, looking for my mooring in the labial tortures and languors of words) be I whatever, it must be obvious that I am an existentialist . . .[41]

Mailer is clearly playing with the problem of voice, of the relation between the writer and the characters he creates. Similarly, the discussion of the identity of his unnamed narrator with which 'Way Out' opens, is in fact a discussion of the author's relation to his fiction and to his reader:

> I must necessarily take into account that the duller minds among you cannot support the luxury of listening to a voice

without a face unless you are handed some first approxi-
mation to my state.[42]

Unable as yet to resolve the problem of voice, Mailer builds the
problem into his fiction (as he had done within the larger unit of
Advertisements for Myself), something which he was to do, in different ways, with all his later fiction.

In his subsequent non-fictional work, *The Presidential Papers*
and *Cannibals and Christians*, the extended sentence with its
blend of philosophical jargon, poetic imagery and obscenity is a
continuing feature of his style. But perhaps the most distinctive
feature of these essays and 'interviews' is the kind of dichoto-
mised metaphorical structure which was visible but not dominant in *Advertisements for Myself*. God and the Devil, hip-square,
totalitarian-existential, instincts and institutions, and foetal
and foecal passages. This taste for dichotomy leads him into
much intellectual crudity, but provides him with a metaphorical framework within which to articulate the more complex and
involuted aspects of his vision; 'Metaphor exists to contain contradiction', as Mailer says in 'The Political Economy of
Time'.[43] Though the intention is clear, too often in *The Presidential Papers* and *Cannibals and Christians*, Mailer's metaphors
contain little but the repetition of attitudes already stated in *Advertisements for Myself*. Certain words like 'totalitarian' (and
'plastic', 'synthetic' and 'mechanical') are repetitiously
employed to describe what Mailer dislikes, the tone is often
dogmatic and irritable, and where the philosophical jargon is
unadorned by imagery or obscenity, it seems pretentious – a
'big' voice assumed for 'universal truths' which amount to little
more than empty generalisations:

> But the war between being and nothingness is the underlying
> illness of the twentieth-century.[44]

Whilst Mailer's intellectual shortcomings can be seen in these
stylistic failures, he seldom exposes himself quite as obviously
as in the above statement. For the most part, in *Cannibals and
Christians*, such statements are followed by an ironic qualifi-
cation or a shift to a different tone. There is no single authorial
voice accountable for the many inconsistencies and ambiguities, but rather a succession of different voices with completely

different intonations and implications.

Among the multiplicity of such tones and voices, it is difficult to identify with any certainty which most closely expresses the attitude and feeling of their author, who stands in the same ironic relation to them all. 'A Speech at Berkeley on Vietnam Day' is an ambitious almost Joycean exercise in this multiple-toned style. The essay opens with Mailer quoting his own review of Lyndon B. Johnson's book *My Hope for America* in which he inveighs against Johnson's 'totalitarian prose', composed of clinical clichés, 'overweening piety', and 'sentences which are nothing but bricked-in power structures'.[45] The essay deals not just with the Vietnam war, the state of America and the personality of LBJ, but offers *itself* as a literary rebuttal of totalitarianism and a blow for the other side – 'variety, dissent and extreme possibility'.[46] He makes his critique of the war stylistically by reproducing in the appropriate mode almost every American attitude towards the war. In colloquial American tinged with obscenity, Right-wing support for Johnson and Johnson himself are ridiculed:

> If there was one thing hotter than Harlem in the summer, it was air raids on rice paddies and napalm on red gooks. Now he had a game. When the war got too good, and everybody was giving too much space to that, he could always tell the Nigras it was a good time to be marching on the White House . . . He could even make all those Barry Goldwater rednecks and state troopers happy – that was a happy nation, when everybody had something going for them. The Nigras had their Civil Rights and the rednecks could be killing gooks. Yes, thought the President, his friends and associates were correct in their estimate of him as a genius. Hot damn. Vietnam. The President felt like the only stud in a whore-house on a houseboat.[47]

Immediately after this comic passage, Mailer moves into an ironically elaborate, formal voice of a lecturer making an exposition of the problem:

> Ladies and gentlemen, you will notice that up to this point, I have offered little in the way of closely reasoned quiet argument. I did observe for myself that in the discussions about

Vietnam which took place last Saturday in Washington, and which were seen by many of us on television, there was an abundance of rational arguments advanced for our escalation in Vietnam and an equal abundance of equally rational arguments against our involvement there.[48]

Besides the stylistic parodies of the redneck and liberal-academic positions, Mailer, in cameo, suggests the tones and attitudes of the psychologist, the business man, the 'average American' towards the war. Shifting from the expository, the prophetic and the scientific to the moralistic tones of the adolescent, he explores this subject through the language in which the essay is written rather than through any lineally developed argument. What might be called a specifically 'Maileresque' style emerges at certain points, but as one voice among many, no more authoritative than the others:

> Something in the buried animal of modern life grew bestial at the thought of this Great Society – the most advanced technological nation of the civilised world was the one now closest to blood, to shedding the blood and burning the flesh of Asian peasants it had never seen.[49]

At the point at which he makes an explicitly political demand (as opposed to the 'visionary'[50] demand for hand-to-hand combat) it is in the declarative tones of statesmanlike reason:

> I say: end the cold war. Pull back our boundaries to what we can defend and to what wishes to be defended. Let Communism come to those countries it will come to. Let us not use our substance trying to hold on to nations which are poor, underdeveloped, and bound to us only by the depths of their hatred for us.[51]

The method of 'A Speech at Berkeley On Vietnam Day' is essentially that of *Why are We in Vietnam?*, the novel he published two years later. The language of *Why are We in Vietnam?* is an attempt to reflect cross sections of American speech, to embody in language the multiple voice of American dream life. It is not, though, the language of rational 'daytime' America, but as DJ makes clear of the subconscious suppressed streams of American thought which the narrator, DJ, can beam in only at night:

if the illusion has been conveyed that my mother, DJ's own mother, talks the way you got it here, well little readster, you're sick in your own drool, because my mother is a Southern Lady . . . she don't talk that way, she just thinks that way.[52]

The richness and suggestiveness of much of this language, stems not merely from the number and variety of idioms and speech rhythms used, but from the wit of their conjunction:

Now, Rusty rolls that Château-Lafite-Mouton-Rothschild around his liver-loving lips, and he can tell 49 from 53 from 59, all the while thinking of 69. He sings the song of the swine, DJ's daddy, nice fellow actually. Also forgot to mention he's an unlisted agent for Luce publications, American Airlines Overseas Division, and the IIR – the Institute for International Research – shit! Spy Heaven they ought to call it.[53]

Here Rusty's move from his 'cowboy fore-ass bears'[54] to the sophistication of his wine connoisseurship is reflected by the sudden shift to the clipped English idiom. Another shift back to the American vernacular registers the political point about American 'research' foundations which cover espionage activities. The expletive 'shit' is introduced to indicate that the extended euphemisms are to be cut short, and the spade is to be given its rightful name – 'Spy Heaven they ought to call it.'

The tones of Harlem, the Evangelical South, Texan Wasp, Eastern Jewish, Eastern English, Midwestern and many other national and regional sub-groups are distinguished and juxtaposed in the same long extended sentence-units, which are sometimes two pages long. Some of the best examples of this technique occur in the use of the Evangelical prayer meeting rhythms in Intro Beep 2; the interjections of 'amen amen' and the invocations to the 'lord' are used to brilliant effect in this mock-solemn disquisition beginning, 'But what then is the asshole of electricity?'[55] One of Mailer's objectives is to recreate in language the contradictions and tensions of American thought, to suggest in this way the reasons 'Why we are in Vietnam'. But further than this, the writing is itself intended to be restorative; the potential energy and creativity of the American language are what may save the nation from the 'communication engineers'[56] of totalitarianism. A close reading of *Why are We in Vietnam?* reveals this deep concern with the medium as itself regenerative, as the 'light' in this *Gotterdammerung*. The language is not therefore merely the most striking feature of the novel, it is this sense the most important – in the vital composite style lies perhaps the only positive of the novel.

The style of *Why are We in Vietnam?* is not only 'very American' it is also very literary.* Where in *The Naked and the Dead* the literary and the colloquial divide into description and dialogue, the purple passages and the 'fuggin', in *Why are We in Vietnam?* the two modes are completely fused. The allusions to Shakespeare and Donne are interlaced with the scatalogical; techniques from the world of popular fiction and comics (the 'Zacks!' and the 'Wows!') are combined with more poetical devices – the puns, allusions, quotations, rhymes, assonance and alliteration. In his role as disc jockey and 'troubadour'[57] DJ ranges from Shakespeare to Batman, taking in large doses of Joyce and Burroughs, and his language is an attempt to contain and unify these disparate elements – 'E Pluribus Unum'. Intro Beep One is a virtuoso exercise in the voice. The first line with its multiple punning ('hole' and 'come'), its assonance, its oblique invocation of Donne, the promise of the trip to come, introduces DJ. His role is dramatised in the style and pace of his delivery, the brash high speed verbalisation of the professional speiler – the disc jockey. The linguistic intentions are explicitly stated and enacted in the form of the statement:

> Let go of my dong, Shakespeare, I have gone too long, it is too late to tell my tale, may Batman tell it . . .[58]

The themes of murder and violence against man and nature are evoked through the allusions to *Macbeth*, and the schizophrenic nature of the narrator is suggested in the Dr Jekyl image. After a densely textured first paragraph, Intro Beep One goes on to introduce most of the major themes of the novel:

* 'He had kicked goodbye in his novel *Why are We in Vietnam?* to the old literary corset of good taste, letting his sense of language play on obscenity as freely as it wished, so discovering that everything he knew about the American language (with its incommensurable resources) went flying in and out of the line of his prose with the happiest beating of wings – it was the first time his style seemed at once very American to him and very literary in the best way, at least as he saw the best way'. *The Armies of the Night*, p. 48.

the preoccupation with technology (Edison), media (McLuhan, broadcasting, tape-recorders, phonographs), the multiple nature of reality ('no such thing as a totally false perception'), sex ('think of cunt and ass'), the condition of America ('the world is going shazam'), existentialism ('we live in dread of God') and death ('Death where is your gates?'). This sample of suggestive confusion (the exact relation of these elements to each other is *not* suggested) ends with a dying fall with a reference to Corinthians and Sing a Song of Sixpence:

> and listen children to your dear old ma, ever notice how blood smell like cunt and ass all mix in one, but rotten, man, the flesh all rotten like meat and fish is biting each other to death, and Death where is your gates, Mother Fucker, are they hot? Big ass tomb, big ass tomb, the fish are in the fireplace and the nerve's begun to sing, make it cool, DJ, make it cool.[59]

These local successes – the experiments with language seem to me both interesting and creative – are offset by the structural incoherence and confusion of the metaphors. While the animal imagery shapes the novel's vision, the electricity and communications metaphors which are used to give the novel its form are not successful. Conceived as a night-time broadcast, relayed by DJ, the novel (apart from the trip to Brooks Range) is what the nocturnal disc jockey picks up and plays back: the suppressed desires, fantasies and impulses of the American unconscious. Mailer sets up an elaborate (and unnecessary) complex of metaphors about magno-electricity fields, radio waves and interference bands to convey the efforts of the writer to penetrate the minds of readers subject to an 'electrox Edison' bombardment from the media. Similarly his attempts to erect metaphorical models for the American psyche in terms of electrical waves and electro-magnetic fields are weaker, crassly scientised versions of the spirits, magic, and supernatural symbols he used in *An American Dream*. In so far as the 200 pages of the novel represent a vision of the American mind, an answer to the question posed in the title, it is a fragmentary and finally minor answer. It represents a falling-off from the controlled integration of theme and form which marks *An American Dream* (1965), Mailer's most achieved novel since *The Naked and the Dead*.

An American Dream, in spite of being written for serial publication, is a unified construction held together by visible themes, symbolic patterns and the expanding consciousness of its narrator. In the discussion of Mailer's heroes in Chapter 1, I outlined a view of Rojack as a hero in quest of rebirth, regeneration in an allegorised but distinctively American world. The violence and the perversion that he encounters in the thirty-two hours of the novel are not merely 'an assortment of dull cruelties and callous copulations',[60] as Elizabeth Hardwick described them. Nor of course are they a realistic description of America, but a poetic representation of the spiritual travails through which Mailer's hero must pass in order to reach a new state of consciousness, a vision of the Celestial City. The allegorical level of the novel places it within the literary tradition of 'dream-visions', and the imagery and symbolism suggest that Mailer's intention was to create a modern pilgrim who is a descendent of Bunyan's and even of Dante's characters. So, for example, Rojack's murder of Deborah and the failure of their marriage is not presented on the realistic or psychological level as Fitzgerald presented Nicole and Dick Diver's marriage in *Tender is the Night*, although later in the novel the relationship between Deborah's destructiveness and her incestuous relation with her father is established. Mailer indicates this level of explanation but does not develop it. In the early chapters of the novel, she is presented primarily in terms of image and symbol: through the Hecate myth, the cave-cellar-darkness images, the animal similes, and the intensive use of olfactory imagery which acts as a comment not on her physical state but her moral function in the allegory. There is, in the terms of the symbolism, a *poetic* justice to her murder, since Rojack's act of violence against her is the symbol of his freedom from failure, hatred and despair.

The development of themes and of Rojack's consciousness takes place in complex patterns of the language, the style registering the situations and responses of the novel's hero. Every incident of the narrative, the killing of the Germans, the murder of Deborah, the sexual encounters with Ruta and Cherry, the fights with Shago and Kelly, is a stage in Rojack's battle with Good and Evil, courage and cowardice, creative and decreative impulses. Thus the writing about sex and violence is a careful,

intensely literary exploitation of such situations, loaded as
Richard Poirier has pointed out with concepts of choice and
salvation. For all its exuberant detail and immediacy, Rojack's
sexual encounter with Ruta is a tightly-controlled contribution
to the design of the allegorical scheme; her body is, literally, his
field of battle, and symbolically the arena in which he struggles
with his conflicting attitudes to the murder he has just committed. The 'prison'[61] of her 'sad womb' represents his assumption of responsibility and the 'Devil's kitchen'[62] of her anus offer
him the possibility of freedom. With Ruta, Rojack chooses the
decreative impulse, the foecal rather than the foetal passage to
spend his 'seed.' Immediately afterwards, inspired by this
devilish influence, he throws Deborah's body from the window,
reports the 'suicide' to the police, and feels 'as fine and evil as a
razor'.[63] When later that evening he makes love to Cherry, he
chooses, as it were, the 'Lord' and in consequence, recognition
and responsibility:

There was no desire to take my pulse. I was a murderer. I
was: murderer.[64]

The description of their love-making is again weighted with
allegorical choices, this time of a positive nature: the similes,
interjections, the clauses which break up and circle round the
main clause, all contained in an extended syntactical structure
rising to the lyricism of the final clause:

I was passing through a grotto of curious lights, dark lights,
like coloured lanterns beneath the sea, a glimpse of that
quiver of jeweled arrows, that heavenly city which had appeared as Deborah was expiring in the lock of my arm, and a
voice like a child's whisper on the breeze came up so faint I
could hardly hear, 'Do you want her?' it asked. 'Do you
really want her, do you want to know something about love at
last?' and I desired something I had never known before, and
answered; it was as if my voice had reached to its roots; and
'Yes,' I said, 'Of course I do, I want love,' but like an urbane
old gentleman, a dry tart portion of my mind added, 'Indeed,
and what has one to lose?' and then the voice in a small
terror, 'Oh, you have more to lose than you have lost already,
fail at love and you lose more than you can know,' 'And if I do
not fail?' I asked back. 'Do not ask,' said the voice, 'choose

now!' and some continent of dread speared wide in me, rising like a dragon, as if I knew the choice were real, and in a lift of terror I opened my eyes and her face was beautiful beneath me in that rainy morning, her eyes were golden with light, and she said, 'Ah, honey, sure,' and I said sure to the voice in me, and felt love fly in like some great winged bird, some beating of wings at my back, and felt her will dissolve into tears, and some great deep sorrow like roses drowned in the salt of the sea came flooding from her womb and washed into me like a sweet honey of balm for all the bitter sores of my soul and for the first time in my life without passing through fire or straining the stones of my will, I came up from my body rather than down from my mind, I could not stop, some shield broke in me, bliss, and the honey she had given me I could only give back, all sweets to her womb, all come in her cunt.[65]

The major themes of the novel are present in this passage: choice and the existential risks involved ('a lift of terror' and 'the continent of dread'), the transcendence of 'will' for something 'deeper', the connections between sex and procreativity. The conception of Rojack's experience as a 'battle' is kept alive in the references to 'arrows', 'shield', 'passing through fire', and in the use of the verb 'speared' and in the simile 'like a dragon'. The positive options in the situation are carefully disposed in the different images of light, sea, honey, and the 'great winged bird'. These work cumulatively so that the orgasm, when it comes, has taken on a whole cluster of symbolic meanings – a surmounting of defences, a 'balm' for Rojack's accumulated bitterness, his 'choice' to love and a celebration of fertility.

Mailer uses yet another kind of style in the two telephone conversations placed strategically in the middle of the novel. Thematically, these stand in contrast to the presentation of Rojack's murder of Deborah, as a dramatic and summary exposure of the poverty of the 'rational' world's reaction to the event. His two employers are no more concerned with the question of moral responsibility and guilt than are the horde of the mediocre and the mad, and their inability to respond to the moral significance of murder is vividly dramatised in realistic dialogue. Before the issue of murder and suicide has been resolved, without Rojack's being charged with any crime, the television company and the university trustees have in effect 'judged' him guilty. The decision to dismiss Rojack is not made on the moral grounds of his having taken human life, but as a piece of expedience – 'the quantity of publicity and the contingent innuendo'[66] – the terms, it is implied, in which the television corporations and universities operate. The substance of both conversations, then, is to inform Rojack of his loss of job, but the mode of the two conversations is nicely differentiated. Mailer represents Arthur's dishonesty and opportunism in the language he uses. The combination of psychologistic clichés with show-biz vulgarisms also established his consanguinity with Herman Teppis, the film producer in *The Deer Park*. Both God and the Devil are dead for Arthur (whose syntax and speech rhythms are recognisably Jewish) and their place has been taken by the Corporation and the Park Avenue analyst's Freud. The passage works as a persuasive indictment of this kind of secular 'rationality'.

The conversation between Rojack and his head of department Tharchman, is another feat of skill – a classic exposure of the liberal dilemma in the face of real moral issues. Tharchman displays much more sensitivity toward his role of mediator between the university authorities and the lecturer he is charged with dismissing, but he actually performs the same functions as Arthur. He is presented as a limited but honourable man:

> he was considered pedestrian, good for keeping the Ph. D. mill a Ph. D. mill. Nonetheless, it must not have been easy for him to grind out his decent portions of salt and meal for each of us. Good old Protestant centre of a mad nation.[67]

Mailer's point in this characterisation is to underline the helplessness of the liberal who works within the system: how can those who refuse or are unable to accept responsibility for their own actions attempt a moral evaluation of others? His liberal principles are betrayed by his professionalism, and he emerges as an apologist for the administration, uncritical of his role in the situation except at a technical level:

> I've managed it (the conversation) abominably. Accept the reality, accept the reality. See it from the University's point of view. Perhaps we feel we've done our honourable best to pay

the indefinable price, and, yes, perhaps gain the even more indefinable benefit of having a creative intelligence in the Department who inspires most respectable people with a deep-seated sense of uneasiness . . .[68]

This short passage recalls the excellent use of dramatic dialogue in *The Deer Park*; Tharchman's initial hesitation and degree of personal feeling are registered in the first three abruptly short sentence-units. His attempt, at an earlier point in the conversation, to dissociate himself from the decision to dismiss Rojack, then falls away and his identification with 'the University' is signalled in the shift from 'I' to 'we'. The 'I' who has managed something badly is subsumed into the 'we' who have done 'our honourable best'. The rhetoricism of the next sentence with its balanced repetition of 'perhaps' and 'indefinable' is the perfect vehicle for the smug liberal sentiment that the department has after all braved the 'deep-seated uneasiness' of 'most respectable people'. The irony is of course that Tharchman is justifying the department on the basis of its past record (in employing 'creative intelligence' at all) on an occasion where it is capitulating precisely from fear of what 'most respectable people' would say.

The third telephone call in this chapter entitled 'A Catenary of Manners' is with a former friend of Deborah's, an extreme example of the forces of irrationality with a supernatural gift of smell. At the plot-level she furnishes Rojack with the information about Deborah's involvement with high-level espionage, thus providing him with a missing link in the chain – a political reason for his escape from legal punishment. Her response to her friend's death and Rojack's situation is confused and incoherent, but in common with the response of Arthur and Tharchman, it is completely devoid of any real moral dimension. The three conversations are carefully organised to reveal the moral vacuum in which the hero exists and also how the conventionally 'sane' reactions of Tharchman and Arthur are as inadequate to Rojack's experience as the semi-mystical extravagances of someone whom Rojack calls 'a very silly little girl'. The sharpness and subtlety with which Mailer establishes these points through realistic dialogue serves to highlight the *deliberate* nature of his decision to use image and symbol to create character in *An American Dream*; it was not an inability to use more traditional techniques which caused him to turn to other conventions, but the inadequacy of traditional, empirical realism for Rojack's view of existence. This point is made very neatly in the confrontation between Rojack and Roberts in the apartment, where the hero suggests that his wife may have committed suicide because she was haunted by demons. 'I don't know how to put demons in a police report', says Roberts. The police report is the equivalent of a style which excludes the demonic, and the exchange between the policeman and the hero reflects Mailer's struggle to evolve a literary style which comprehends these elements, which moves beyond what Tony Tanner calls a 'narrow naturalism'.[69]

An American Dream is not of course simply an allegory about a modern American pilgrim; the novel also draws on the conventions of popular fiction, the first-person narratives of Fleming, Spillane and Dashiell Hammett. The two-dimensionality of the characterisation, the absurdity of the pulp-fiction plot with its unhappy playboy hero, torchsinger, available maid, shrewd detective and heartless financier are obvious enough; these banalities of plot and characterisation are elements deliberately borrowed from the popular detective story and are best understood, I think, as an extension of the popular-serious antithesis which is set up within the story of Rojack's life. Rojack makes the point early in the first chapter that he straddles the worlds of popular and 'serious' values:

> There are times when I like to think I still have my card in the intellectual's guild, but I seem to be joining company with the horde of the mediocre and the mad who listen to popular songs and act upon coincidence.[70]

His position is what makes his 'dream', his experience uniquely relevant for both halves of the split consciousness of the American mind. Mailer's point in exploiting *simultaneously* the serious novelistic convention of the 'dream-vision' and the techniques and conventions of pop-fiction is to draw attention to the gap between the 'guild' and the 'horde'. In *The Presidential Papers*, he consistently makes the point that for the majority of Americans popular fiction, films and television programmes determine the quality of their dreams, that the American psyche is based on fantasies of sex, normal and perverse, and violence in every form, from simple murder to Goldfinger's complicated tortures. To write another 'serious' novel without representing these elements would be to fail 'to clarify the nation's vision of itself' and fail in the mammoth job he set himself of 'making a revolution in the consciousness of our time'.

Mailer's attempt, as I see it, is precisely to embody his moral seriousness in the passages about sexual violence, to pose his view of sanity, creativity and health in a form which would be accessible to a mass readership. Behind his complaints that 'it is journalism rather than art which forges the apathetic consciousness of our time'[71] lies a continuing insistence that the novel must provide an experiential solution to the ills of America. The breadth of this ambition is visible in the title he chose for the novel. *An American Dream* refers the reader to *the* American dream – that phrase which embodied the frontiersman's aspiration in the early days of the Republic, the hopes of the immigrants who flocked to America in the nineteenth century and the early part of the twentieth, the dream of equality, democracy and individual fulfillment, in fact the dreams both material and spiritual of the 'good life'. In choosing his title therefore, Mailer drew on a phrase which has a political, cultural and literary history, a phrase resonant with meanings.

If the very title suggests the scope of his intention, the first paragraph of the novel sets up questions about the literary form, the question of 'fiction' and whether this is to be a fictive piece at all:

> I met Jack Kennedy in November, 1946. We were both war heroes, and both of us had just been elected to Congress. We went out one night on a double date and it turned out to be a fair evening for me. I seduced a girl who would have been bored by a diamond as big as the Ritz.[72]

The tone is that of a fictionalised autobiographical piece written for a magazine and it contains all the elements appropriate to the genre – sex, status, wealth. It signals to the reader with expectations of a traditional realistic novel, that this is not what is being attempted. The metaphor which closes the paragraph is of course the title of a story by Scott Fitzgerald and besides being hyperbolic in a manner appropriate to magazine fiction, it asserts the novel's relation to a literary predecessor who also attempted to treat 'the American dream'. But if the book is not a realistic narrative of events, neither is it the popular success story that this opening seems to promise. One of the ironies of the title is that Rojack's story is an inversion and critique of the American dream of power and success.

In the second paragraph, Rojack describes Deborah's father's path to success in traditional American terms: from a 'poor hick Presbyterian'[73] family of Irish immigrants, he made a million (200 times) and married into a family with another kind of advantage – political and social power. Rojack repeats the pattern by marrying Deborah to achieve the same kind of 'dream' ('she had been my entry into the big league'[74]) but kills her to achieve a different kind of power, to break out of the dream world. Each of the other characters has his own variation of the dream: Ruta, from a Berlin slum, wants to blackmail the millionaire Kelly into marriage (the female version of making a million is to secure a man who has already done it); Ganucci, once a poor Sicilian, has succeeded in the Italian style by becoming a leader in the Mafia; Shago's ambitions are expressed through music and sex, as a jazz singer and 'stud', the variant of the dream available to a Harlem Negro; Cherry has a poor white Southern girl's dream of becoming a 'lady' by whatever means; Roberts and Leznicki, the Irishman and the Pole, enact their dreams of power and success as American cops. The crucial difference between Rojack's dream and that of the other characters, what enables Mailer to present his fantasies of sex and violence as 'heroic', is that although *the* American Dream has turned into a nightmare of materialism, his dream remains authentically spiritual. He has abandoned his early dreams of political power and Presidential office, and is not primarily interested in money, power or prestige:

> 'God,' I wanted to pray, 'Let me love that girl, and become a father, and try to be a good man and do some decent work.'[75]

At forty, having decided that he is a failure in his own terms, he is in quest of nothing less than regeneration, a new life.

To identify this moral impulse in the novel and to trace the articulation of that vision through image and symbol, does not, clearly, obviate criticism of the morality thus presented. But one of the effects of the novel's double existence as it were, as thriller and fable, has been to produce criticism which tackles one level or another, but which fails to hold both in focus. This is, I think, partly because of the ambiguities of this double form and partly because of the absence of any authorial voice; Rojack's consciousness dominates the book and it is difficult in the absence of any critical authorial voice not to assume idenification between the author and the narrator. The mysticism-rationality theme raises this problem in a fairly typical way. Rojack's marriage to Deborah had merely confirmed a susceptibility which dates from his war-time experience: his killing of the four Germans, his courage and escape from death, are not explicable in rational terms, and 'his too large an appreciation of the moon'[76] began there. The description of the event is loaded with sexual and religious concepts which are worked out in the rest of the narrative. The possible Christian and Jewish explanations (his parents' beliefs) are no longer viable for him, and he reverts to a (historically) more primitive religious cult – he postulates a supernatural agency and identifies this with a particular totem, a full moon. This moon religion with Deborah's occultism and Cherry's Manicheanism represent the religious (or superstitious) pole of the faith-reason dichotomy:

> After nine years of marriage to her I did not have a clue myself. I had learned to speak in a world which believed in The New York Times: Experts Divided on Fluoridation, Diplomat Attacks Council Text, Self-Rule Near for Bantu Province, Chancellor Outlines Purpose of Talks, New Drive for Health Care for Aged. I had lost my faith in all of that by now: now I swam in the well of Deborah's intuitions; they were nearer to my memory of the four Germans than anything encountered before or since . . . Yes, I had come to believe in spirits and demons, in devils, warlocks, omens, wizards and fiends, in incubi and succubi.[77]

The above passage suggests the limitations of the other pole of the reason-faith dichotomy; the headlines of a national newspaper are a curious example of the world of rationality. Rojack, it is clear, is not deserting any great intellectual system when he succumbed to Deborah's 'well of intuitions'. For an 'excessively

bright'[78] intellectual to imagine that newspaper headlines
might illuminate an individual's experience of killing four men
is excessively naive, or the dichotomy is a false one. At a
moment of revulsion against his private religion, Rojack describes the alternative again:

> I wanted to be free of magic, the tongue of the,Devil, the dread
> of the Lord, I wanted to be some sort of rational man again,
> nailed tight to details, promiscuous, reasonable, blind to the
> reach of the seas.[79]

Rojack's image of the 'rational' man is as limited and idiosyncratic as his personal faith. What for example, from the
evidence of the novel, is specifically rational about pro-
miscuity? Despite the existentialist terminology, the hero's
quest for salvation and the moral theme generally, are not satis-
factorily realised in this false dichotomy. But if the rational
alternatives to mysticism are presented in an unreal and distorted way, the question arises as to whether Mailer is presenting them thus to indicate that his hero is capable of seeing them
in a more meaningful and realistic way. The other possibility is
that Mailer is offering the reader a dichotomy which he himself
feels is valid. There is no clear indication *from the text* where the
author stands in relation to such points, although from Mailer's
other works it is possible to believe he does accept such ideas.
Although such ambiguities do not finally mar the novel's real
achievements – Rojack's experience is ultimately a pretext for a
stylistic exploration of Mailer's many contradictory ideas –
they suggest that Mailer's problems with 'voice', the identification or distance from the 'I' of his novels, have not yet found
a resolution.

VOICE

The omniscient voice of *The Naked and the Dead* was, as I have
suggested earlier, borrowed from other writers whose social
vision Mailer found congenial at the time. When he abandoned this vision, he also discarded the traditional vantage-
point of the author with regard to his fiction. In *Advertisements
for Myself* he recognises and discusses the problem of the
writer's relation to his work, and focuses in particular on the
difficulty of finding a representative voice, of devising a hero

able to voice his creator's ideas about the world:

> For six years I had been writing novels in the first-person; it
> was the only way I could begin a book, even though the third-
> person was more to my taste. Worse I seemed unable to
> create a narrator in the first-person who was not overdeli-
> cate, oversensitive, and painfully tender, which was an odd
> portrait to give because I was not delicate . . .[80]

He goes on to describe how, during the publishing problems
with *The Deer Park*, he started to re-write the novel in a specific
attempt to cope with the problem of 'voice':

> I was now creating a man who was braver and stronger than
> me, and the more my new style succeeded, the more I was
> writing an implicit portrait of myself as well. There is a
> shame in advertising yourself that way, a shame which
> became so strong that it was a psychological violation to go
> on.[81]

These comments throw considerable light on Rojack, the
hero-narrator of the novel he wrote nine years after *The Deer
Park*. The problem of the insubstantiality of the narrators of
Barbary Shore and *The Deer Park* stems, in Mailer's view, from the
dissimilarity between author (Mailer himself) and narrator. At
the time of *The Deer Park* the only solution that he could see, that
of making his narrators an 'implicit portrait' of himself, was difficult for him to accept. In *Advertisements for Myself*, he overcomes
his 'shame' and decides to use his personality as 'the armature
of the book', and the decision has a crucial influence on his later
work. With Rojack he 'shamelessly' exploits his own characteristics and ideas, and achieves the unity of vision and voice
which was lacking in his second and third novels – certainly
Rojack is a more consistent and central creation than either
Lovett or O'Shaughnessy of *The Deer Park*. But the creation of
narrator-heroes so close in many ways to their author raises
certain new questions in both *An American Dream* and in the earlier story, 'The Time of Her Time'. In *The Naked and the Dead* the
author maintains distance between himself and his characters,
any identification takes place between the omniscient author
and the reader. They share a 'secret communion' about the
characters, a knowledge which is greater than the characters

possess about themselves. In *An American Dream* and 'The Time of Her Time' however the reader has no authorial attitude to guide him in how he sees Rojack or Sergius, since Mailer has deliberately chosen to present a reality mediated entirely through the consciousness of his narrator, with none of the distancing devices of authorial comments, irony etc. This use of subjective realism ('le realisme brut de la subjectivite'[82]) gives the maximum intensity to Rojack and Sergius' fantasies which a more distanced treatment would make impossible, but it makes evaluation of their experience problematical.

In 'The Time of Her Time' O'Shaughnessy's experience with Denise Gondelman is presented through his consciousness of the situation. Not only is there no direct authorial comment, there is no implied position to which the reader can relate. How for example does the reader respond to O'Shaughnessy's self-evaluation?

> I was the messiah of the one-night stand, and so I rarely acted like a pig in bed, I wasn't greedy, I didn't grind all my tastes into their mouths, I even abstained from springing too good a lay when I felt a girl was really in love with her man. . . . Yes, I was a good sort, I probably gave more than I got . . .[83]

Does one take this statement at its face value, as an honest and realistic description of a man who is limited but is in fact 'a good sort'? Or as an exposé of the fatuous complacency of a destructive male chauvinist who is unable to relate to women except in sexual athletics? The passage and perhaps the story as a whole is ambiguous. The technique of 'authorial silence' is generally used so that the reader's response to character is not mediated by another's (i.e. the author's), and the reader is forced to confront his own values and assumptions without further intellectual or moral guidance from the author. The novelist using this technique not only refuses to 'play God to his characters'[84] but refuses to play author for his readers. The justification for this theory of the novel rests on the belief that whilst authorial control was acceptable in the past, in the present where shared values and assumptions are impossible, the correct thing for the author is precisely to throw the reader back on his own assumptions. To suggest a world view common to writer and reader would be to create an illusion of moral certainties and shared values, and would therefore be deceptive. In 'The Time of Her Time' particularly, but also in *An American Dream*, Mailer achieves a unity of voice and statement but at the expense, I think, of exposing his work to many conflicting readings. The devotee of Mickey Spillane's fiction will respond to Rojack and O'Shaughnessy's sexual exploits very differently from the way in which Kate Millett responds in *Sexual Politics*, but both these extremes of readers would have difficulty in understanding *from the text* where Mailer stands in all this. Mailer uses authorial silence not primarily to confront his readers with their lack of their shared assumptions, but as a way of coping with his own ambiguities and his lack of a coherent position about many of the issues he raises. He implicitly admits this when talking about Forster and the problem of voice in the *Paris Review* interview, reprinted in *Cannibals and Christians*:

in some funny way Forster gave my notion of personality a sufficient shock that I could not manage to write in this third person. Forster, after all, had a developed view of the world; I did not. I think I must have felt at that time as if I would never be able to write in the third person until I developed a coherent view of life. I don't know that I've been able to altogether.[85]

In the interviews and 'dialogues' in *Cannibals and Christians* Mailer develops a new tactic to cope with the lack of a coherent view of the world. He creates an interviewer and a persona called Mailer who, in 'The Metaphysics of the Belly' and 'The Political Economy of Time', discuss all Mailer's preoccupations from the nature of aesthetics, scatology, cannibalism, food, form, time, death and the soul. The dual voice enables him to dramatise, often humourously and usually paradoxically, his 'incoherent' ideas on these subjects. This split authorial voice assumes the form of a self-confrontation and directly prefigures the method he was to use in *The Armies of the Night* and his two subsequent books. Almost any exchange in the sixty-three-page interview, 'The Political Economy of Time', serves to illustrate this method at work:

Mailer: They show themselves in every crack of every detail in our lives, in the processing of our food is one seat of the plague and in the plastic commodities we handle, the odor of vaginal jelly, the dead character of public communication, the pollution of air, the collective assaults upon human nerve.

Interviewer: Are these the criteria? or merely temporary technological trials? – just a list of your familiar prejudices?

Mailer: Look at the forms. The forms of the modern world break down. That is where you find all objective criteria – in the art of the twentieth century, above all in the architecture, in the empty monotonous interchangeable statements of our modern buildings.

Interviewer: Not all that again! Not all this reduced to still one more of your endless diatribes about modern architecture.

Mailer: I'm talking not of architecture but of form. Form is the deepest clue we possess to the nature of time in any epoch, to the style of the time, to the mode by which reality is perceived in the time, to the way time moves in the consciousness of man, where it possesses grace, where it is hobbled, how strength addresses itself to weakness.[86]

The statements of the 'Mailer' of this interview are, first of all, an excellent exercise in self-parody; Mailer exposes his obsessions, his intellectual and stylistic tics to the rebukes of his alter ego 'interviewer' and absolutely deadpan, goes on to justify himself in the statement on form. It is of course not just a statement about form in general but about his own work and the form of this 'interview' in particular. 'Architecture' in his essay work is often a metaphor for artistic 'forms' which are in turn metaphors for 'the style of the time'. His thesis, as it is presented in the 'Argument' for the interview, is that although science was founded on the metaphor, 'the twentieth century has shipped metaphor to the ghetto of poets' and 'experiment has replaced the metaphor as a means of enquiry'.[87] His project is to take metaphor out of the ghetto and back into intellectual life as *the* tool with which to examine subjects generally left to the scientist; cancer must no longer be left to the medical scientists, personality to the psychoanalysts, America to the social scientists, nor electricity to the physical scientists, but they must be recaptured as the terrain of the novelist and writer.

The associational stream of images, the contradictions which accumulate within his metaphors and similes ('Metaphor exists to contain contradiction'[88]) are intended to be a reassertion of the function and powers of metaphorical language.

Why are We in Vietnam? seems to me again primarily an assertion of Mailer's notions about language; if 'form is the deepest clue we possess to the nature of time in any epoch'[89], then the explanation for America's involvement in Vietnam must be sought in the language, the 'form' of the times. DJ's voice is in fact a cross-section of American speech, a multiple voice not of rational 'daytime' America but of the streams of American thinking generally suppressed. Ranald Jethroe, self-styled genius and 'shit-oriented late adolescent'[90] is this metaphorical voice of America, the 'I' who addresses the reader in the Intro Beeps and who describes in the third-person present historic the adventures that befall DJ, character and hero. As narrator he is omniscient by virtue of his role as 'Disc Jockey to the world'[91], and as a professional verbaliser he is a symbol for the novelist and writer. The voice is continually and aggressively calling attention to itself as problematical; is it that of a Harlem Negro freak hallucinating that he is a rich white Texan boy or vice versa – that of a shade dreaming he is a spade. Lest the reader forget this lengthy opening debate, he is reminded that 'there's no security in this consciousness'[92] and again on the final page is told that 'you never know what vision has been humping you through the night.'[93] The 'form' of the narrative is also raised as a question by DJ; is it stream of consciousness, memory, fantasy, imagination, drug-induced hallucination, documentary or fabricated (fictionalised?) tape recordings? Questions of form are continually and somewhat heavily placed before the reader:

> The fact of the matter is that you're uptight with a mystery, me, and this mystery can't be solved because I'm the centre of it and I don't comprehend, not necessarily, I could be traducing myself. Por ejemplo, the simple would state that Intro Beep I is a stream-of-conch written by me . . .[94]

The language of *Why are We in Vietnam?*, DJ suggests, is not definable in the conventional terms of literary criticism, and his personality as narrator is not reducible to psychological categories:

> he's a humdinger of latent homosexual highly overhetero-
> sexual with onanistic narcissistic and sodomistic overtones, a
> choir task force of libidinal cross-hybrided vectors.[95]

All these things yet none of them, DJ is created as an American Everyman and (the word 'choir' makes the point) a chorus. Like Shago Martin, his voice is 'not intimate but Elizabethan, a chorus, dig?.[96] Considered as the recreation by means of language of Mailer's ideas about America, the book achieves a great deal; but even with this flexible, imaginative composite voice, Mailer fails to produce a literary construct which in any sense measures up to his enormous ambition, the scope of which is again visible in his title.

Mailer does not attempt to repeat this voice experiment in *The Armies of the Night*, but moves back for the first time since *The Naked and the Dead* to the third person, but a third person with a difference. He makes himself the hero of the book in an attempt to create a voice which comprehends the first person of his essay work but gives that 'I' a fictional existence, a dimension beyond the autobiographical, by creating a character called Norman Mailer. The book's subtitle, 'History as a Novel – The Novel as History', indicates the nature of the undertaking. The attempt is to write both a history of and a novel about the anti-Vietnam War march in Washington in October 1967 – and in doing so to make certain points about the fictional and historical modes. The first section of the book (History as a Novel) is, in his own words, 'nothing but a personal history which while written as a novel was to the best of the author's memory scrupulous to facts'.[97] In the second section (The Novel as History) Mailer uses a more historic style to write what in fact develops into a kind of 'collective novel'[98] about the battle of the Pentagon. Apart from the narrative occasion, the march and the battle, *The Armies of the Night*, as I see it, iş a culminating point in Mailer's literary history; it is another volume in the muted autobiography of Norman Mailer which runs through his work, an essay at the big novel about America which has been his proclaimed ambition to write for the last ten years, and further than this it is a reaffirmation of the novel as a form and a philosophical justification of the 'novelistic' approach to experience.

Seen as an experiment with 'voice', as an attempt to bridge the fiction-autobiography, novelist-reporter dichotomy which had dominated his work for more than a decade, *The Armies of the Night* seems to me a brilliant effort. His 'Mailer' creation gives him a subjective vantage point from which to expound his most pressing concerns but at the same time forces a new distance into the expression of those ideas. He is able to write about the problems of America as he sees them with a new flexibility and irony – the stridency which marks so much of his essay work is absent from *The Armies of the Night*. The 'historical' narrative is enriched (with no loss of actuality) by the deft use of various novelistic devices, as in the major's speech in 'A Palette of Tactics'. After a thorough use of newspaper, radio and first-hand reports to establish the facts of the confrontation between troops and demonstrators, Mailer departs from the 'fetish with factology'[99] and inserts an imaginery briefing speech into the mouth of the officer in command of the troops:

> . . . the point to keep in mind, troopers, is those are going to be American citizens out there expressing their Constitutional right to protest – that don't mean we're going to let them fart in our face – but the Constitution is a complex document with circular that is circulating sets of conditions – put it this way, I got my buddies being chewed by V.C. right this minute maybe I don't care to express personal sentiments now, negative, keep two things in mind – those demos out there could be carrying bombs or bangalore torpedos for all we know, and you're going out with no rounds in your carbines so thank God for the ·45. And first remember one thing more – they start trouble with us, they'll wish they hadn't left New York unless you get killed in the stampede of us to get them. Yessir, you keep a tight asshole and the fellow behind you can keep his nose clean.[100]

Through this creative reconstruction, a device commonly used in classical historiography, Mailer characterises people and motivations which would remain anonymous in traditional reportage. His characterisation in *The Armies of the Night* – of himself, Robert Lowell, Dwight McDonald and other public personalities – is humorously perceptive; the host of minor characters, the students, the Marshal and the Nazi, his fellow jailbirds are vividly and economically drawn. The frequent diversions from the narrative into the ruminations and reflections of his hero upon what is taking place, are diversionary only in the narrowest sense. The behaviour and preoccupations of Mailer are an integral part of the strategy of the book since an exposure to the subjectivity of the hero-narrator is, in the author's estimate, the real key to an objective 'historical' assessment of the events described.

The relation between fiction (the Novel) and a report of these events (the History) is of course one of the major themes. Mailer expounds his theory of this relation in the chapters entitled 'A Novel Metaphor' and 'A Palette of Tactics' but it also runs through the treatment of his hero's career as a writer. His twenty years as a writer have produced two extremes of response, conflicting sets of expectations and opinions which 'Norman Mailer' who is sensitive to these things, is vividly aware of. At one pole he is seen as the gifted novelist of *The Naked and the Dead* who has gone astray and who should give up his journalistic excursions into extra-literary fields and concentrate on writing a *serious* novel. Mailer has been intermittently attracted by this view of himself; he refers to work on a 'big novel about America' in *Cannibals and Christians* and subsequent interviews, and when approached by Goodman about the march on the Pentagon, responds very much in this spirit:

> When was everyone going to cut out the nonsense and get to work, do their own real work? One's own literary work was the only answer to the war in Vietnam.[101]

If one's vocation is simply 'literary work', then the writer clearly should limit himself to doing his 'own real work' and not involve himself in practical political activity. But Mailer had already taken a position on writers who limit themselves to a 'partial vision'[102] and determined that his own vision should be more comprehensive. At the other end of the critical spectrum there are those who see this attempt at comprehensiveness as journalistic and who therefore see Mailer primarily as a journalist. His resentment at this view of his work is dramatised in the scene at the Liberal Party in Washington; Robert Lowell tells him that he thinks him 'the best journalist in America' and Mailer's retort is significant:

> 'Well, Cal,' said Mailer, using Lowell's nickname for the first time, 'there are days when I think of myself as being the best writer in America.'[103]

The use of the word 'writer' (*not* novelist) is, I think, Mailer's assertion of a unity in his literary activity which takes in both fiction and journalism and transcends the categories of 'art' and popular writing. *An American Dream* was an attempt to bridge the gap between the serious novel and popular fiction and *The Armies of the Night* makes the same attempt in relation to journalism and the novel. As Rojack theorised about the need to make connections between the 'intellectual guild' and the 'horde of the mediocre and the mad' who are the overwhelming majority of Americans in his view, so the hero of *The Armies of the Night* (who, like Rojack, is a writer astraddle the intellectual-pop distinction) sees his primary responsibility as making connections between 'the two halves of America . . . not coming together'.[104] Musing on the problem on his way to the Occoquan jail, Mailer exposes once again his literary intentions and his conception of the function of the modern *writer*:

> . . . and Wolfe dead too early and Hemingway a suicide – how much guilt lay on the back of a good writer – it grew worse and worse. As the power of communication grew larger, so the responsibility to educate a nation lapped at the feet, new tide of a new responsibility . . . It was an old argument and he was worn with it – he had written a good essay once about the failure of any major American novelist to write a major novel which would reach out past the best-seller lists to a major part of that American audience brainwashed by Hollywood, TV, and *Time*.[105]

Within the deliberations on fiction and history, which are basically an expansion of the argument in *Cannibals and Christians* about metaphor's superiority over scientific enquiry, Mailer reaffirms his faith in the novelistic approach. The tasks of the writer may have changed, but his methods still hold good. In 'A Novel Metaphor' he expands this point at some length; he refuses to believe in scientific history on the epistemological grounds that it has not developed a strictly scientific methodology – this idea is put forward in the metaphor of the telescope and the tower. History, in a philosophical sense, is as much a fiction as is a novel. An attempt at a historical coverage of the march on the Pentagon would be unscientific because the bias of the cameramen and the reporters negates the neutrality of the instruments they use. Further the mediation of the human element is concealed in the apparent neutrality of their technical equipment. In contrast to these 'historical' methods, a novelistic treatment within which the bias of the novelist and his beliefs is exposed as fully as possible, at least permits the subjective element to be understood and allowed for. His second theoretical justification of fiction is made in 'A Palette of Tactics' where he points out that a historical approach to an event like the Pentagon march must always be 'exterior' whereas a novelistic treatment can deal with the interiority of the events and the people involved in them:

> the novel must replace history at precisely that point where experience is sufficiently emotional, spiritual, psychical, moral, existential, or supernatural . . .[106]

History in Mailer's definition is either pseudo-scientific or external, and when it goes beyond this, it is itself novelistic. This elaborate philosophical justification of the novelist's methods must I think be taken as itself metaphorical – an interesting and central part of the characterisation of the novelist-hero – rather than judged by the stricter criteria of logic. In a more specific sense it explains Mailer's presentation of the comic-hero, 'Mailer', who is the protagonist. His egotism, the detailed description of the nuances of his thinking and behaviour, is not to be taken as evidence of the author's exhibitionism, but is part of Mailer's belief that a writer must fully expose his authorial position to enable the reader to understand and be 'educated' by his work.

The Reporter in *Miami and the Siege of Chicago*, Aquarius in *A Fire on the Moon* and the Prisoner in *The Prisoner of Sex* can be seen as creations in the same mode. As recently as 1965, in the *Paris Review* interview, Mailer seemed still to hope that if he could develop a sufficiently 'coherent view of life' he could write fiction in the third person where the artist,

like the God of creation, remains within or behind or beyond
or above his handiwork, invisible, refined out of existence, in-
different, paring his fingernails.

In his latest work Mailer has completely abandoned such an
attempt, and *The Armies of the Night* outlines his reasons or
rationalisations for doing so. Lacking the distance or discipline,
some critics would say, to remain 'behind' his handiwork in the
tradition of the modern novel, he has developed a new aesthetic
of the novel where the author must be at all times 'visible', exposed and central to his fiction. For some, this development
constitutes not a new form of novel; but an autobiographical enterprise, an abandonment of fiction itself. Whilst this is not, it
seems to me, true of *The Armies of the Night*, Mailer's new conception of fiction and the author's role within it, has serious
limitations. *A Fire on the Moon* and *The Prisoner of Sex*, which are
both about the technologising of human existence, reveal one of
the central flaws of this method; anchored in the author's personality and ideas, his literary work can become only an infinite
series of variations on the same themes and characters which
(as *The Prisoner of Sex* already suggests) leads to repetitiousness.
Originally designed to release the author from the limitations of
a single authoritative authorial voice, to give him a maximum
freedom in dealing with the contradictions and nuances of the
culture in which he lives, his new aesthetic methods may lead
not to greater comprehensiveness and imaginative freedom, but
to a rigid and confining circularity. And since it is Mailer's
vision which is too 'big' for any voice other than his own, his difficulties and failures rest with himself as a writer as much as
with his times.

The 'muscular' style which he found first in 'The White
Negro' has developed considerably since the mid-fifties, yet is
still recognisably the basis of his present literary work. In his
latest books this style is pushed to its farthest limits; the long
extended sentence structures often fall into incoherence with
the strain of carrying his hyperbolisms, the involuted
metaphysical symbols, the rhetoric of prophetic cultural
generalisations and ironic self-parody. The dichotomous
metaphorical structures through which he approaches nearly
all experience have become as rigid as the 'totalitarian prose of

the communications engineers' which they were originally evolved to explode. There are indications in his most recent work that this style is becoming exhausted and that Mailer as a writer is aware of this fact.* The obvious question that he faces is then whether to continue writing an even more ornate and decadent variation of this style with the self-imposed task of changing the world through his writing, or whether he can break out from this pattern. There are as yet few signs of a possible new voice or style, and it is possible of course that Mailer will turn to a different medium – such as film-making or practical politics – to achieve his ambitions. Yet given his chameleon literary history and the fact that it is still his ambition to write 'the great American novel',[107] the exhaustion of his present style may represent merely another turning-point, a marking time, as it were, before plunging into fresh literary endeavours.

---

* 'He had been left with a huge boredom about himself. He was weary of his own voice, own face, person, persona, will, ideas, speeches, and general sense of importance.' (*A Fire on the Moon*, p. 5) Mailer is here referring specifically to his political activities in the mayoral campaign, but the comment seems to take on a larger significance within the book. See also his comment in *The Armies of the Night*, p. 188, on his boredom with 'totalitarianism'.

4 'The Prisoner of Sex'

In Mailer's work the treatment of sexuality and the relation between the sexes has become closely, indeed inseparably, linked
with his ideological and metaphorical 'war' on totalitarianism.
Nevertheless, because sexual matters have become increasingly
important in his writing, particularly since *The Deer Park*, and
because this aspect of his work has aroused a great deal of critical comment, it is perhaps worth looking at it as a separate
theme. The relation between men and women has been present
as a theme from his first novel, but like his political outlook and
his stylistic development, his treatment of it seems to me to
undergo considerable changes in the mid-fifties, around the
time of *The Deer Park* and *Advertisements for Myself*. When the
socialist ideas which dominated his first two novels 'failed' for
Mailer, he turned on the one hand to existentialist ideas and on
the other hand returned to certain nineteenth-century
progressive traditions. From both of these he drew fairly
eclectically on everything which seemed to provide him
with ammunition for his crusade against totalitarians and
the technologising of human existence. The 'organic' tradition, on which he drew fairly heavily from *Advertisements
for Myself* onwards, contained certain attitudes towards
women, sexuality and procreativity which are to be found
in all his subsequent work and which find their apotheosis in his
book, *The Prisoner of Sex* (1971). Certainly neither Reich, nor
Sartre and the other existentialists, provided him with the ideas
about women which begin to emerge about this time –
although, of course, there are other contemporary ideological
influences which reinforce the organic view of sexuality.

In one respect, Mailer's literary treatment of sex is

consistent. From *The Naked and the Dead* to *The Prisoner of Sex* the relation between men and women and the sexual act are always 'significant', that is, significant of other things. Whether it is used to symbolise the degree of alienation in social relations, the decadence of a totalitarian state, the possibilities of good and evil, or the metaphysical relation to 'Time', the individual's sexuality and specific sexual experience almost always stands for something other than itself. There are few if any passages in Mailer's work, where sex is allowed even a relative autonomy, where a sexual experience between a man and a woman is described as simply as pleasurable, or not, for the individuals concerned. Criticism of his recent work as 'reactionary' in terms of sexual politics has to take account of the fact that he has always used sex in a highly stylised symbolic way, sometimes to expose, sometimes to endorse, sometimes ambiguously simply to describe the male attitude to women.

In his first novel, *The Naked and the Dead*, the competitive virility cult, in which the American male is held prisoner, is subjected to searching and detailed criticism; it is one of the key elements of the author's indictment of American values. Although the effects of these sexual standards on women as a group are outside the scope of a novel about war and an army, there is sufficient indication in the portraits of the men's wives and girlfriends, of its negative effects on their lives and relationships. Although Mailer later explicitly 'takes sides' with his own sex in what he describes as the 'brutal bloody war'[1] between the sexes, in his first novel the criticism is of attitudes and the institutions which maintain them, there is <u>no hostility</u> <u>towards women</u> as a social group.

One of the five 'choruses' in the novel is devoted to male attitudes toward women; in the form of a dramatised conversation between several of the platoon members, Mailer underlines the hostility and contempt which many of the men feel towards women:

Brown: . . . Okay. While we're home, and slipping a little meat to them every night they're all lovey-dovey. Oh, they can't do enough for ya. But the minute you go away they start thinking . . .

What do you think your girlfriend is doing now? I'll tell you what. It's just about six a.m. now in America. She's wakin' up in bed with a guy who can give her just as much as you can, and she's giving him the same goddam line she handed you. I tell you, Minetta, there ain't one of them you can trust. They'll all cheat on you.

Polack: There ain't a fuggin' woman is any good.[2]

The chorus is in effect a confrontation between the twin sides of the American male's attitude to women; stereotyped romanticism and cynical hostility. Brown and Polack ridicule Stanley and Minetta's half-hearted defence of their sexual partners, not maliciously, but in an attempt to give them the benefit of their experience as 'men'. Except perhaps for Goldstein and Ridges, the concept of *human* experience and relationships does not exist for them; the world is divided into men and 'women' and relations between the sexes are discussed in terms of sex: sexual needs, sexual prowess and sexual fidelity. The point, which is made in numerous conversations between the men, is that women exist primarily as 'sexual objects'; particular objects belong to particular men but this ownership is threatened by the woman's possible sexual activity with other men – which constitutes betrayal or cheating on the woman's part and theft on the part of the other man. All the soldiers, even the younger romantic ones, implicitly accept a sexual double standard, the male's need and right to unlimited sexual activity and the necessity for the woman to belong sexually to only one man. Within this common ground there exist nevertheless considerable variations in attitude and experience which Mailer explores in some detail.

The younger, unmarried men like Wyman and Minetta accept the general distrust and contempt for women but insist that their own girlfriends and their own experience are exceptional:

Aw, it was different with us, Red. It was *really* something special.[3]

The more bitter of the men explain the passing of the romantic view of women and love in terms of women's innate deceit and badness, and Red sees it in terms of social pressures – 'the arguments, the worries over money, the grinding extinction of their youth'[4] – but Mailer manages to suggest the self-defeating nature of romantic love itself. Both Wyman and Minetta express their most positive feelings about their girlfriends in terms of their own image, the woman's love is the reflection and tribute to the man's merit, actual or potential:

> Claire really made me feel I could be something. After a date, I'd leave her, and walk around for a while by myself, and I don't know, I just *knew* I was gonna be a big guy someday.[5]

Their appreciation of the woman is measured in terms of this hazy self-aggrandisement, and neither Rosie nor Claire is seen to have any independent qualities which make her admirable or lovable. Their disappointment in love is inherent in the terms in which they see it. The older or longer-married men who have been forced to come to terms with the fact that they have not made it as the 'big guy', that they are ordinary and no woman's love can change that fact, feel bitter and deceived by the reality of married life. Since love and a particular woman's love had seemed to promise some way out of this, their resentment and disappointment is directed at their one-time hope of escape, at their partner in romantic illusions.

Those who have come through the romantic stage make their different adjustments to women and sex. Their ambiguous attitude to women's sexuality is expressed in the complaint both that 'women just aren't interested in it',[6] and when they meet women of whom this cannot be said they respond by calling them 'whores'. Whether defined as frigid or promiscuous, women are seen as threatening, deceiving, disappointing and the men in different degrees are all bitter, cynical or resigned. For Brown, the bitterness about his own wife is expressed in the sexual exploitation of other women, sex with whom only confirms his view that they're 'all fuggin whores'.[7] Polack who shares this view but without the same personal bitterness, uses it as a justification for exploiting them on a financial basis, working as a part-time pimp before being drafted. Wilson, the platoon womaniser, uses women to gratify his sensual appetites and, except when his wife asks for some of his army pay to support their children, maintains a benignly appreciative attitude towards them. Apart from Wilson, Red is one of the older members of the platoon who appears to feel no particular hostility toward women, and has had at one time a reasonably satisfactory relationship lasting several years. Understanding that it is not the woman's fault that love does not solve personal and economic problems, he nevertheless fails to take issue with the others' attitude, just as he fails to challenge their anti-semitism although he does not share this either.

In the 'Time-Machines', the chorus on women, and the conversations throughout the narrative, the novel presents an uncompromising picture of the destructiveness of conventional sexual roles and of the virility cult in particular. It depicts the frustration and fears of inadequacy that the fetishism of sexual performance inflicts on men and the divisive and damaging effects that this has on men's relationships with other men. The only unifying feature, with which the soldiers console each other, is their common contempt for women as a group; and here Mailer manages to suggest the analogies between racism and sexism at the psychological level. However oppressed, inadequate and ordinary the men feel – 'there's not a damn thing special about any of us, not about Polack, or you or Stanley or me. We're just a bunch of GIs'[8] – they can always feel superior to women. Gallagher's hatred of Jews is shown as his attempt to cope with the fact of economic and social failure in a society based on the success-ethic; Brown, Polack and Martinez's hatred and contempt for women compensates them psychologically for their disappointments about other aspects of their lives. This point is made most explicitly in the 'Time Machine' about Martinez:

Little Mexican boys also breathe the American fables.[9]

For Mexicans brought up in the Spanish quarter of Texan towns, almost totally excluded from the dominant White Anglo-Saxon Protestant culture, their ability to feel superior to their own women cushions them from feelings of failure and inadequacy, whilst they express their aspirations and revenge against the dominant culture in the desire to 'screw' Wasp women:

I screw white Protestant girls, firm and aloof.[10]

The two Jewish members of the platoon have different

attitudes towards women partly, Mailer suggests, because of their greater respect for the family and for woman's central role within the family. Goldstein speaks with warmth of his wife, despite their sexual difficulties, and accentuates the value of 'companionship'[11] within marriage. Both Goldstein and Roth admit privately that they dislike and feel threatened by the sexist attitudes of the other men; but although they do not reduce women to the level of being merely 'sexual objects' for men, they both accept that women's 'differentness' from men makes a woman less than a man as regards intellectual interests:

> These thoughts he had were the kind of things you could tell only to a man. A woman had to be concerned with her children, and with all the smaller things.[12]

The only other voices raised against the prevailing hostility and contempt for women (Ridges is for the most part silent during these discussions) are those of the younger men still involved in some form of romantic love. Mailer carefully suggests the limited and transient nature of Minetta and Wyman's defence of women through his portrait of Gallagher. After a courtship in which the woman is seen through a blur of romantic idealism and hopeful egotism – 'He would defend the lady in the lavender dress with his sword'[13] – Gallagher is unable to sustain much affection for his wife in the reality of living together with her:

> She used to wear a tight hair net in the house, and always of course her habit of sitting around in a slip which had a frayed edge. Worst of all was something he had never quite admitted to himself; the walls of the bathroom were thin and he could hear the sounds she made. She had faded in the three years they had been married. She didn't take the right care of herself, he thought, bitterly. At this moment he hated the memory of her . . . .[14]

Through the characterisations of Croft and Cummings, Mailer suggests the extremes to which the cult of masculinity points. For both, women are secondary human beings, symbols for the power struggle which takes place between men – as

Cummings expresses it with classical economy and restraint:

> The average man always sees himself in relation to other men as either inferior or superior. Women play no part in it. They're an index, a yardstick among other gauges, by which to measure superiority.[15]

Although women thus conceived play no part in the struggle, the violence and hostility appropriate to a combat situation is present in Croft and Cummings' attitude towards them. Both think and talk of women as 'bitches' and 'whores'; for both men the sexual act is an act of aggression, an act of symbolic struggle where the domination of the woman stands for the domination of the inferior by the superior power. Thus Croft as a lover resembles Croft the hunter and fighter:

> His ancestors pushed and labored and strained, drove their oxen, sweated their women, and moved a thousand miles. He pushed and labored inside himself and smoldered with an endless hatred.
> (You're all a bunch of fuggin whores.)
> (You're all a bunch of dogs.)
> (You're all deer to track.)[16]

Similarly, Cummings's sexual passion is shown to be the form of another more vital rage for power which once identified for what it is by the woman, nullifies all her sexual feelings for him and effectively destroys their marriage:

> Their lovemaking is fantastic for a time: He must subdue her, absorb her, rip her apart and consume her . . .
> Margaret is kindled by it for a time, sees it as passion, glows and becomes rounded, but only for a time. After a year it is completely naked, apparent to her, that he is alone, that he fights out battles with himself upon her body, and something withers in her.[17]

Both Croft and Cummings' wives, becoming aware how they are being used, turn to other men for consolation and revenge in the only way open to them. Mailer's exposé of this process, of how the deadlock of mutual bitterness and resentment in the couple is reached, is clear and comprehensive. Equally clearly, he shows how Croft and Cummings are not only warlike in sex, but see war and violence as sexual: from the 'thrill'[18] of his deer-hunting expeditions as an adolescent, to the 'excitement'[19] of killing his first man (as a National Guardsman breaking a strike), to Croft's experience of violence and killing in the war – which, as Mailer carefully establishes, gives him physical sensations closely resembling sexual pleasure and orgasm. In a more abstract sense the same point is made about Cummings' experience and his attempts to find common symbols for warfare and sex in the curve of the parabola:

> of a man or woman's breast, the fundamental curve of love, I suppose. It is the curve of all human powers . . . and it seems to be the curve of sexual excitement and discharge, which is after all the physical core of life . . . It is the curve of the death missile as well as an abstraction of the life-love impulse.[20]

This connection between sex and violence, between the energy of the sexual act and the excitement and energy involved in violence and killing, is an ongoing concern in Mailer's work. With hindsight, it is easy to trace many of the later formulations and images of sex and violence back to this early treatment. But while Mailer has admitted his 'secret admiration' for violent people like Croft,[21] and while one can detect in *The Naked and the Dead* a fascination with ideas about sex and violent action, one cannot claim that the position Mailer expounds in his later work was already latent in his first novel. In *The Naked and the Dead* these ideas are presented critically as part of neo-fascist, totalitarian ideology. There are ambiguities in this presentation undoubtedly, but on balance the novel, it seems to me, takes a humanistic view of the sexual questions it raises, exposing and analysing both the male virility cult and the destructive effects which 'male chauvinist' attitudes towards women have on the man, the women and their relationships.

The relations between men and women is not nearly so central a theme in *Barbary Shore*, Mailer's second novel; what sexual relationships there are between the six characters serve mainly as statements about the political issues at stake. Certain aspects however suggest a continuing interest in sex and sexual relations beyond the needs of the political allegory; besides a fair amount of contingent discussion between McLeod and Lovett on the subject, and Lovett's memory of a sexual experience during the war which unites 'love with artillery shells and sex of polished steel',[22] this centres mainly round the characterisations of Guinivere and Monina. Whereas in *The Naked and the Dead* Mailer attacks the stereotyping of the male role, in *Barbary Shore* he attacks the cult of female sexuality as fostered by mass entertainment and Hollywood in particular. Guinivere at one level is a symbol of the apolitical masses whom all ideologues need for the success of their systems, but she also embodies a specious sexual promise for Lovett, McLeod, Hollingsworth and Lannie Madison. The nature of her sexual appeal is suggested at the beginning of the novel:

> Her thin lips pursed, but this was beneath the other mouth of lipstick which was wide and curved in the sexual stereotype of a model on a magazine cover, and seemed to work in active opposition to the small mobile lips beneath.[23]

Her reality ('the small mobile lips beneath') is the opposite of the image she presents to others; this is Mailer's most immediate point. But in the working-out of the novel, it becomes clear that the other characters want her neither for her 'real' sexual self nor for the 'sexual stereotype' she presents, but as a substitute for what each of them want or need. For McLeod, who married her, she offered protection from those who were looking for a single man but also a substitute for an abstraction:

> All my life I've loved ideas. So I loved the idea of loving my wife.[24]

For Hollingsworth, with whom she runs away, she is a sexual substitute for her husband, exciting because she has been his (McLeod's) sexual partner. Lannie sees her as a symbol of goodness and beauty, who can impart those qualities to her, if she will allow Lannie to be her 'mirror' of love. Lovett comes nearest to actual sexual desire by casting her in the role of 'the nymphomaniac'.[25] Mailer's point seems to be that not merely is the woman a false stereotype of the sexual object, but that most sexual desire is not properly sexual at all.

The perversion of sexuality is accompanied by a perversion of the characters' emotional capacities generally. Again Guinivere is used to symbolise this in the 'love story' that she tells Lovett and in her treatment of Monina – whose name suggests the monadic nature of the 'onanists the world is forever shaping'.[26] Hoping to take her to Hollywood as a child star, Guinivere deliberately stunts her mental and physical development to that end. What she produces is a grotesque parody of the American female child, a nymphet who performs a ritualistic dance signifying the relations between the sexes in America – 'a parody of amorous advance and retreat'[27] – and is 'an interpreter'[28] of her mother's love story. The presentation of both Guinivere and Monina reveals the strongly moralistic element in Mailer's imaginative handling of his theme. This moralism is also evident in the suggestion of homosexuality in Hollingsworth's characterisation. As with Cummings in *The Naked and the Dead*, Mailer uses sexual deviation to symbolise negative qualities in both Lannie and Hollingsworth, as he himself commented in *Advertisements for Myself*:

> Part of the effectiveness of General Cummings in *The Naked and the Dead* – at least for those people who thought him well-conceived as a character – rested on the homosexuality I was obviously suggesting as the core of much of his motivation. Again, in *Barbary Shore*, the 'villain' was a secret police agent named Leroy Hollingsworth whose sadism and slyness were essentially combined with his sexual deviation.[29]

His attitude towards homosexuality in his first two novels, once recognised, seemed in contradiction with his otherwise libertarian ideas, and he resolved to eradicate those attitudes as far as possible from his future work. In the same essay, 'The Homosexual Villain', reprinted in *Advertisements for Myself*, Mailer explained how he revised the characterisation of Teddy Pope in *The Deer Park* in line with his new distaste for equating homosexuality with villainy. In the revised version of that novel, Teddy Pope's homosexuality is still a symbol for negative social forces, his mannerisms are caricatured in the traditional ways that heterosexual novelists generally caricature homosexuals, but he is nevertheless presented sympathetically. He is shown, as in the scene in which Teppis tries to force him to marry Lulu, capable of honesty and affection in contrast with the hypocritical morality of the 'straight' world represented by Teppis. The homosexual in Mailer's third novel is no longer the agent, the striking force, of totalitarianism, but is another victim.

The Deer Park is 'totally about sex' and also 'totally about morality'[30] but there is no total, unified view of either sexuality or morality. Instead there are a number of ideas which range from the essentially humanistic strictures on the commercial exploitation of sex to the 'existentialist', near-nihilist position of the practising pimp, Marion Faye. Sexuality is again used as an index of other things, in this case integrity in work and politics and the individual's heroic potential, and at the more general level it is used to symbolise the moral state of the nation. The novel attacks the prostitution of sexuality both in itself and as the incarnation of the prostitution of ideas and emotions which takes place in Hollywood. Desert D'Or is as full of the 'depravity, debauchery and all the vices' that Mouffle D'Angerville found in Louis XV's Deer Park, as Mailer's epigraph makes clear. Since the resort, and the film industry it serves, are presented as the place where American morality – its myths and attitudes – is manufactured, Mailer is in a sense taking his critique to the heart of the matter. Where in *Barbary Shore* he showed the effects of this 'morality' in the portraits of Guinivere and Monina, in *The Deer Park* he attempts to show not merely effects but also the causes for what he sees as the widespread corruption of American life. His analysis is not in itself very original, however competent (and at times brilliant) the fictional treatment of this material. The morality of Hollywood films is corrupt, the novel suggests, because it is a morality dictated by the profit motive and the ideological purposes of a politically repressive state.

The first chapter describes the physical aspects of the resort and, as with the image of Guinivere's two mouths, stresses the conflict between appearance and reality:

> It was a town built out of no other obvious motive than commercial profit and so no sign of commerce was allowed to appear.[31]

The moral condition of its inhabitants is suggested in the darkness and dimness of its bars and clubs, and the lack of clear moral distinctions is symbolised in the basic confusion of day and night:

> Above the serving bar with its bank of bottles, its pyramids of

citrus fruit, a smoky-yellow false ceiling reflected into the mirror behind the bar and coloured the etching of a half-nude girl which had been cut into the glass. Drinking in that atmosphere, I never knew whether it was night or day, and I think that kind of uncertainty got into everybody's conversation.[32]

The Hangover, which Sergius starts to frequent, exemplifies the confusions and uncertainties of the town. In the absence of any other moral and political ideas, Dorothea and her friends live by the values and standards of the musical and the melodrama; her patriotism and her attitude to men – 'There were good guys, bastards and phonies'[33] – are the stock-in-trade of the 'imaginery world' which Sergius opposes to the real world 'where orphans burned orphans'.[34] Despite his grasp of this distinction between the real world and the world of simplistic fantasies, Sergius falls in love with one of the queens of the imaginery world – the movie-actress, Lulu Meyers.

Structurally their affair stands as a parallel to that between Eitel and Elena, and as the means whereby Sergius attains enough knowledge about the imaginery world to reject it in a more final sense than he has yet been able to. Lulu is thus the temptress, the beauty queen who represents some of the most alluring aspects of the Hollywood world; when he rejects her (after she has already rejected him as a sexual partner), this, along with his refusal of a job in that world, stands for his rejection of the illusory world in favour of 'reality' – earning his living at various menial jobs and later becoming a writer. Lulu herself is presented as a symbol for how the film world uses women, as both bait and victim. She is the perfected sex-object, the beauty-queen 'actress' who represents the ultimate of desirability for the mass audiences of men and women who want to possess her or become like her. She is an adult version of Monina in *Barbary Shore*, with, as Sergius discovers, a kind of infantile passive sexuality beneath the mythic attractions of her blondeness, her 'little turned-up nose, dimpled chin and pouting mouth'.[35] She acts out the same 'parody of amorous advance and retreat'[36] that Monina does, before giving herself sexually to Sergius:

How long it went on I do not know, but it was a classic. She coaxed me forward, she pushed me back, she allowed me a strip of her clothing only to huddle away like a bothered virgin. We could have been kids on a couch.[37]

Having become her lover, the struggle is not over, each sexual act is a ritual battle and test whereby the possessing male proves his manhood:

What she may have intended as a little dance was a track and field event to me, and I would snap the tape with burning lungs, knotted muscles, and mind set on the need to break a record. It was the only way I could catch her and for three minutes keep her. Like a squad of worn-out infantrymen who are fixed for the night in a museum, my pleasure was to slash tapestries, poke my finger through nude paintings, and drop marble busts on the floor. Then I could feel her as something I had conquered, could listen to her wounded breathing, and believe that no matter how she acted at other times, these moments were Lulu, as if her flesh murmured words more real than her lips. To the pride of having so beautiful a girl, was added the bigger pride of knowing that I took her with the cheers of millions behind me . . . I knew I was good when I carried a million men on my shoulder.[38]

In this passage Mailer makes explicit the nature and meaning of the act for the man making 'love' to a sexual object; it is sport, it is war, it is the test and proof of manhood for an imaginary audience composed of the millions of men who desire her image on the screen. Whatever attitude of the author lies behind this passage, however closely Mailer sympathises with his hero's attempt to 'conquer' his sexual partner, the 'information' presented in the text is unambiguous; the woman here is the opponent, the enemy whom the man (like an 'infantryman' who will 'slash', 'poke' and destroy beautiful objects in the conditions of war) must fight and conquer. As it happens, Sergius loses his prize to an even better fighter, Tony Tanner, who is more brutal and all-conquering than the hero. When Sergius reappears in 'The Time of Her Time' he has lost his inhibitions and succeeds in 'putting his mark'[39] on Denise Gondelman in a way which the Sergius of The Deer Park fails to do with Lulu.

In Eitel and Elena's affair, the partners manage to move

beyond this kind of sexual activity, and Mailer treats this
period as a gain, as positive compared with Sergius' battles and
games with Lulu:

> The act was now quiet to them, it was tender – that was the
> emotion he felt over and over – their first nights together
> which he had thought so extraordinary seemed like no more
> than a good hour in a gymnasium compared to what they
> had now.[40]

They cannot sustain this tenderness however for reasons which
were discussed in the chapter on Mailer's heroes. Besides this
use of the affair to symbolise Eitel's failure as an artist, Mailer
makes many of his most interesting statements on sexual relations in his treatment of what happens between the two. Of all
Mailer's women characters, Elena Esposito is perhaps the most
important because he presents her both as a woman but also as
a personality with problems and potential of the same order as
his male characters. She exists, in other words, not merely as a
secondary human being who is an index of others' moral possibilities, but who has herself a moral nature with distinctive
ideas and possibilities for self-development and growth. Because of this, *The Deer Park*, whatever else it is, is in fact what
Mailer called it:

> [the] . . . painful story of two people who are strong as well
> as weak, corrupt as much as pure, and fail to grow despite
> their bravery in a poor world, because they are finally not
> brave enough.[41]

Mailer has not before or since depicted a relationship between a
man and a woman so fully – and the fullness and strength of the
portrait stem directly, I think, from Elena's characterisation
as first human and only secondarily a woman. She, along with
Sergius and Faye, is endowed with heroic qualities which Eitel,
despite his intelligence and courage, finally lacks. She achieves
her 'human' quality and her heroism partly by relinquishing
the advantages of the conventional woman:

> When she loved she kept nothing with which to bargain and
> so she would always lose.[42]

Although she does finally 'lose', in the sense of losing Eitel's love, she never loses his respect for he is forced to recognise that she is in his own terms the more heroic character of the two.

> The essence of spirit, he thought to himself, was to choose the thing which did not better one's position but made it more perilous. That was why the world he knew was poor, for it insisted morality and caution were identical. He was completely of that world, and she was not.[43]

She suffers at his hands because she will not put safety or security before moral considerations – and she can therefore refuse his offer of marriage, although she loves him, because it is his way of settling accounts when he has stopped loving her. When Eitel accepts the security of a return to making professional films, she leaves him for Faye and, after one suicide attempt, begins a destructive descent into prostitution and drinking. Although, as Kate Millett suggests, the moral logic and aesthetic unity of the novel properly require that it end in Elena's suicide[44] (prompted by Faye's search for the ultimate experience of driving someone to their death), Mailer instead chooses to end the novel with her in an empty marriage with Eitel. Even so, the last chapter shows her resisting Eitel and her analyst's attempts to adjust her to being merely the wife of a successful movie director, and Eitel pays tribute to the possibility that she has outgrown his help:

> for she had come now into that domain where her problems were everyone's problems and there were no answers and no doctors, but only that high plateau where philosophy lives with despair.[45]

Not many of Mailer's women characters make it onto that 'high plateau'; if Eleanor Slovoda, Denise Gondelman, and the Elena of the play version of *The Deer Park* – or indeed any of Mailer's fictional women – are measured against Elena Esposito, it can be seen how reduced these later women characters are in comparison with her. She represents the nearest approach to a 'heroine' in the whole Mailer *oeuvre*.

Mailer manages to dramatise many male attitudes to women and sexuality in his treatment of Eitel and Sergius, but leaves those of his third hero, Marion Faye, rather shadowy. His militant anti-humanism, and his desire to purge all 'sentimentality' from human relationships certainly operate against the women he encounters – but they also operate against his male friends, of course. However, women being by cultural definition the more emotional sex, Faye holds them in especial contempt. His outlook and position in Desert D'Or force him early into casually exploitative sexual relationships and into a financial exploitation of his mother. When she refuses to support him any longer, he uses women in the resort as a source of an income and occupation, by becoming a part-time pimp. Of Mailer's early male characters, he most resembles Polack in *The Naked and the Dead*, whose trade and cynicism about love he shares:

> Love was the subject which steered Faye. 'You look,' he said to me, 'you take two people living together. Cut away all the propaganda. It's dull. The end. So you go in the other direction. You find a hundred chicks, you find two hundred. It gets worse than dull. It makes you sick. I swear you start thinking of using a razor. I mean, that's it,' he said waving a finger like a pendulum, 'screwing the one side, pain the other side. Killing. The whole world is bullshit. That's why people want a dull life.'[46]

In his own sexual life he is completely devoid of the vanity and jealousy which characterises Eitel's sex life. With Eitel Mailer is at pains to describe the mystification and egotism which surrounds all his sexual experience but particularly his middle-aged affair with Elena:

> Like most cynics he was profoundly sentimental about sex. It was his dream of bounty and it nourished him enough to wake up with the hope that this affair could return his energy, flesh his courage, and make him the man he had once believed himself to be.[47]

Eitel's 'dream of bounty' is not far removed from Wyman's adolescent view of sex as a dream of becoming a big guy, and it is this kind of romanticism which Faye is out to destroy.

Mailer uses Faye's rigorous perception of the sentimentality and corruption in relationships to comment on both Eitel and Sergius' affairs and attempts to suggest the inverted idealism which directs Faye's apparently sadistic and exploitative treatment of women and people generally. Thus in contrast to

Eitel's self-indulgence and sentimentality with Bobby the call-girl, Faye ruthlessly takes it upon himself to destroy her il-lusions of being in love with Eitel, to crush her vanity 'like a roach' and 'to burn into her brain the seed of what she had never possessed: one grain of honesty'.[48] Faye, then, is the cynic in revolt from sentimentality who in the process of stripping sex of romanticism and sentiment, strips it of all emotional content. Mailer presents Faye's confused and destructive puritanism ambiguously – seeming to suggest at times that it represents a serious and meaningful alternative to Hollywood senti-mentality, and not merely the inverted and punitive image of what it opposes. The kinds of values which emerge from his treatment of Eitel and Elena's relationship – the potential equality between men and women, the possibility of love which is neither gymnastics nor dull dependence but is compatible with the creative work and the honesty that Faye values so highly – are too complex and tentative to provide Mailer with durable positives. Instead it is Faye's position, which in *The Deer Park* is merely the *negation* of liberal humanism (because that is capable of prostitution by the totalitarians of Supreme Pictures), which forms the basis of the sexual attitudes of the hipster. It is possible, I think, to see this development as yet another consequence of Mailer's view of himself as a writer at war with his culture, a writer who is totally committed to a lone, heroic struggle against what he calls 'the totalitarian tissues of American society'.[49] His fear of being disarmed in this battle leads him into an exaggerated rejection of ideas which might be described as compromise or which could be incorporated into the dominant ideology. *Advertisements for Myself* is the story of a writer at war, who becomes convinced that with sex as with everything else, he must explore the extremes of experience and attitudes, to avoid defeat and surrender:

> There was a frontier for my generation of novelists. Coming out of the orgy of the war, our sense of sex and family was torn in two. The past did not exist for us. We had to write our way out into the unspoken territories of sex – there was so much there, it was new, and the life of our talent depended upon going into the borderland.[50]

The extreme implications of Faye's attitudes to relationships and sexuality are visible in 'The White Negro' and 'The Time of Her Time'. But the much earlier story, 'The Man Who Studied Yoga', written in 1952, also reveals, very clearly, the relation between Mailer's theories about sexuality and the growth of his ideas about instincts generally. One of the flaws of the story is the anonymous, omniscient narrator and his comments on the marriage relationship of Sam and Eleanor Slovoda; there is an uneasy relation between the tone of this unnamed authoritative voice and the excellently dramatised conversations between Slovoda and his wife and friends. The marriage relationship is closely observed and generally well-presented, and throughout the story a balance is maintained between irony and sympathy at their lives of 'quiet desperation-cum-psychoanalysis', as Diana Trilling calls it. The voice of the narrator interrupts this third-person presentation to generalise and comment explicitly on what is being presented; thus, their marriage and Eleanor's role in it, is used to present general reflections on the married state and on women:

> No matter how inevitable, I am always sorry when love melts into that pomade of affection, resentment, boredom and occasional compassion which is the best we may expect of a man and a woman who have lived together for a long time.[51]

About Eleanor the narrator says:

> At those times when I do not like Eleanor, I am irritated by her lack of honesty. She is too sharp-tongued and does not often give Sam what he needs most, a steady flow of uncritical encouragement to counter the harshness with which he views himself. Like so many who are articulate on the subject, Eleanor will tell you that she resents being a woman. As Sam is disappointed in life, so is Eleanor. She feels Sam has cheated her from a proper development of her potentialities and talent, even as Sam feels cheated. I call her dishonest because she is not so ready as Sam to put the blame on herself.[52]

Thus the concrete and detailed treatment of Sam and Eleanor's relationship is used to support the narrator's general conclusion about love and marriage – which the reader may well feel it does not, necessarily. The 'inevitability' of love becoming what it has in the case of Mailer's two characters has *not* been established in the story, and yet the narrator's statement is presented as though it had. This kind of tendentious statement about love, marriage and women is allowed to stand without any indication from the author of a critical distance from his narrator; in such instances, and there are several in Mailer's work of this period, it seems fair to assume that the tendentiousness is the author's own.

In the treatment of the characters' reaction to 'The Evil Act', the pornographic film which Sam and his friends watch, the narrator makes a number of comments about their response which, again, I assume to be close to Mailer's own attitudes. The Rossmans, Sperbers and Slovodas are aroused by the film but repress their excitement by talking and joking about it; this fact is presented as a criticism of middle-class intellectual behaviour, as an example of their dishonest and cowardly refusal to 'perform the orgy that tickles at the heart of their desire'.[53] There is a certain appeal in this attitude (which recurs several times in *Advertisements for Myself* and again in *The Presidential Papers*) but it seems to me finally reductionist. If Denise Gondelman has sexual problems, then she should work them out sexually with Segius the Village stud and not discuss them with her analyst, it is suggested in 'The Time of Her Time'; if the Slovodas and their friends titillate themselves with pornographic films, then they should work out their lusts at the physical level and not talk away their desire, the narrator suggests. Mailer shares the Lawrentian objection to sex as 'mental thrills' which may in itself have some validity, but he retreats into a fundamentalist solution which rests on the crude and misleading dichotomy between thinking and feeling. The fact that psychoanalysts deal with patients' problems only at a verbal level, may mean that the problems are contained at this level and, as Mailer suggests is the case with Denise Gondelman, actually inhibit their resolution. But it would be behaviourist to suggest that sexual activity in itself can solve problems which exist at the emotional and psychological level as well. Neither Denise nor indeed Sergius, experiences sex only at the genital or physical level; Sergius gives her her first experience of 'time', her first 'vaginal' orgasm, but obviously her sexual problems are far from resolved. And since the couple do not have, nor want, a relationship which comprehends all the other possible levels, she must return to the 'oral perversions' and her analyst. Sergius has won the distinction of being remembered by her as the man who gave her an orgasm (at the cost of her dislike and his exhaustion) but he has not provided a real alternative to psychoanalytical treatment. The story provides ample evidence of the fact that Sergius' sexual activity is as much of an 'ego-trip'[54] as is Denise Gondelman's talk of Eliot and her complexes, but Mailer, trapped in his opposition between the intellectual and the sexual, seems unable to acknowledge as much. Similarly in 'The Man Who Studied Yoga', it would not resolve the Slovodas' and the Sperbers' problems, nor prove them more honest or authentic if they had an orgy after the film, but only less complex as people.

The descriptions of the sexual act dominate 'The Time of Her Time' and are, I think, excellent dramatisations of a certain kind of relation between men and women. Using tactile and olfactory imagery with tremendous skill, Mailer succeeds in making the sexual activity both vivid and immediate and at the same time creates the lyrical violence of the lovers' attitudes. The male experience – the concentration on performance and energy – is conveyed by the continual use of metaphors from the world of sport, boxing, bull-fighting and athletics. The emotional atmosphere is suggested in the images of combat and confrontation which accompany the most intimate gestures of the sexual act. Although these elements are presented at greater length and explicitness, they are basically similar to the descriptions of sex which one finds in Mailer's early fiction. The differences between the earlier treatments and what one finds in 'The Time of Her Time' is primarily a question of presentation, of authorial identification. In *The Naked and the Dead* and *Barbary Shore* these male attitudes were associated with the authoritarian, politically reactionary characters like Croft, Cummings and Hollingsworth. In *The Deer Park* the anarchistic hero Sergius has a violent and embattled sex-life with Lulu, but this is largely treated as the result of Lulu's character as a Hollywood sex symbol, as a sexual games-player herself. The tension between them and Sergius' violent attempts to subdue her are not presented as a natural or heroic state of affairs, and further, moments between Eitel and Elena are allowed to stand in contrast. In 'The Time of Her Time' the

narrator is permitted to present his nightly struggles in the loft
– and his lack of emotional commitment to his sexual partners –
as a normal if not natural condition for sexual activity. The
hero's attitudes and experiences are presented entirely through
his own consciousness of them, and (given the antisemitic,
'male chauvinist' elements in this consciousness) the authorial
silence becomes oppressive and unsatisfactory. Again and
again the critical reader is forced to question the reliability of
the narrator, but there are no clear signals *in the text* – in the
form of authorial comment, or in the images and symbols –
which denote the author's distance from his narrator's statements.

From external evidence however (from Mailer's other work
of this period and his subsequent statements on sexuality and
women) it is easy to construct a fairly plausible reading of the
story. Mailer as a 'libertarian socialist' is not simply giving a
sympathetic portrait of the triumph of a destructive woman-
hating sexual athlete, but is exploiting the sexual situation to
make certain statements about the forces he sees at work in
American life generally. The battle and the triumph of the male
are intended to be largely symbolic; Denise Gondelman is
slapped, abused – 'You dirty little Jew' – and defeated not primarily because she is a woman but because she represents a
group or tendency which Mailer wishes to see destroyed: the
liberal, middle-class, Jewish intellectuals who have turned
their backs on the primitive instinctual life and have become
part of American totalitarianism. Sergius' triumph as a male is
also symbolic. He is the 'messiah' not merely of the one-night
stand, but of the primitive, the life of the body rather than the
mind. Thus when Sergius calls his sexual mastery of Denise
'the domination which was liberty for her',[55] he is referring to
much more than the reactionary notion that a woman's freedom lies in her submission to a man. By giving her first experience of what he calls 'Time', he symbolically forces the rational,
jargon-infested, totalitarian America to submit to the instinctual freedoms of the hipster.

Nevertheless, even when the symbolic meanings of the story
are recognised, the implications of using one sex (or one race) to
symbolise certain negative values deserve critical comment.
Most contemporary American novelists including Mailer have

rejected the practice of nineteenth-century fiction writers who consistently used Negroes to symbolise evil. At the present time, any attempt to exploit the racial tensions between black and white, to embody the defeat of evil in the defeat of a black man by a white for example, would constitute a major artistic error, since symbolism in the last instance depends on cultural assumptions for effectiveness, for recognition and verification. Mailer's use of women, in 'The Time of Her Time' and in his later work, after he had rejected his earlier fictional practice of using homosexuals to symbolise negativity and evil, suggests that he is finally the 'sexist' that critics like Ellman and Millett have found him to be. To serve his war on totalitarianism, or rather to provide him with the literary villains and the symbolic situations from which to conduct his literary campaign, Mailer has shown himself prepared to exploit sexual prejudice and to make divisions between the sexes serve his aesthetic needs. This is not however to suggest that the sexual attitudes found in his work from this period are merely the result of literary opportunism; the anachronistic sexual ideology is itself a part of the larger anachronism – the infatuation with organicism which I discussed in the chapter on Mailer's politics.

'The White Negro' is Mailer's intellectual and literary manifesto of this period. In it he sets out all the polarities which his conception of life as battle or war force upon him: consciousness and the unconscious, mind and body, institutions and instincts, totalitarian and hip. The essay is an attempt to construct a philosophy, a justification and strategy for his new hero, the American hipster. The hipster is conceived in a time of war, the war against 'the State as l'univers concentrationnaire'[56], and his instincts are his means of survival and his chief weapon. The orgasm is celebrated by the hipster because it is the highest point, the epitome of the life of the instincts which the State has not yet brought under its control and which might lead to the overthrow of the Denise Gondelmans:

> But to be with it is to have grace, is to be closer to the secrets of that inner unconscious life which will nourish you if you can hear it, for you are then nearer to that God which every hipster believes is located in the senses of his body, that

trapped, mutilated and nonetheless megalomaniacal God who is It, who is energy, life, sex, force, the Yoga's *prana*, the Reichian's orgone, Lawrence's 'blood', Hemingway's 'good', the Shavian life-force; 'It'; God; not the God of the churches but the unachievable whisper of mystery within the sex, the paradise of limitless energy and perception beyond the wave of the next orgasm.[57]

The reference to Lawrence is particularly interesting since there are remarkable similarities between Mailer's mythicised hipster (Negroes) and Lawrence's mythicised instinctual heroes (Mexicans and Sicilians). Both writers were concerned with the perversion and restriction of individual possibilities by social structures and both initially use the perversion of sexuality as symptomatic of larger social disorders. They both move from social criticism into a search for the psychic causes of social attitudes and begin to concentrate their hopes on the psycho-sexual level: on the 'peace that comes of fucking'[58] and 'the paradise of limitless energy and perception beyond the wave of the next orgasm'. Both Lawrence and Mailer look backwards to more primitive, pre-industrial societies where they find models for more harmonious, authentic sexual roles and relationships.

The implications and limitations of the organic approach to sexuality and women become apparent in *The Presidential Papers* and *Cannibals and Christians*. The hispter in 'The White Negro' is thoroughly male; if Mailer conceives of women in pursuit of 'limitless energy and perception' he makes no mention of them. The instincts which are celebrated in *Advertisements for Myself* seem to be exclusively the property of the man, and women have separate and quite different imperatives:

> The fact of the matter is that the prime responsibility of a woman probably is to be on earth long enough to find the best mate possible for herself and conceive children who will improve the species.[59]

This kind of biological determinism, which by implication completely excludes women from the political and intellectual advantages gained in the twentieth century, is obviously anachronistic. It is consistent with an earlier image of women in terms

of their 'natural' functions, their role in an organic social
system where the woman had little or no control of biological
factors. To recapture the harmonious relation between man
and woman, Mailer would destroy precisely those developments – like contraception and abortion – which threaten the
existence of the 'natural' relations between the sexes. In this
respect he is completely consistent; he stands opposed to the
technologising of human existence, at the point of production
and reproduction. The diaphragm and the pill are part of the
technological innovations which he sees as responsible for the
present state of America and the industrialised world. Further,
devices which free women from their child-bearing role are responsible for the development of independent, competitive
women with intellectual pretensions of their own – and therefore also responsible for many of the tensions between the two
sexes. Therefore, women who do not make their 'prime' responsibility that of finding a good mate and 'improving the species'
through their children, but who like Elena Esposito set their
sights on the 'high plateau' of general human problems,
become symbols of destructiveness, images for the forces which
Mailer's later heroes must combat and subdue. (Rojack's attitude toward Deborah in *An American Dream* in many respects
recalls Birkin's response to Hermione in *Women in Love*.) Militant about the need for an existential conception of *man's* life
and potentialities, Mailer is blatantly essentialist where
women are concerned. Where his male characters are presented with the right and the necessity to choose their destiny,
women who attempt to do the same are presented as evil and
destructive; *their* salvation it is implied, lies in a return to *their*
'natural' instincts, *their* biologically determined social roles.
His opposition to the ideas of women's liberation in the late
sixties is foreshadowed in the essays of *Advertisements for Myself*
and *The Presidential Papers*; these ideas threaten the liberation
Mailer conceives for women – 'the domination which was
liberty'.

The emphasis on orgasm in 'The White Negro' is replaced
in the essays in *The Presidential Papers* by an equally urgent emphasis on procreation. Not only are contraception and masturbation 'bad'[60] but all sexuality whose end is not ultimately to
conceive children has become negative and wasteful. Purely

hedonistic attitudes towards sexual activity threaten the natural and inseparable relation between sexuality and procreation. World population problems and the problems for women
who have to cope with these 'natural' children are unimportant
beside the need to uphold this principle. When Mailer's inter-
viewers object to the illogicality of Mailer's position – the
wholesale rejection of certain technological and scientific ways
of controlling 'nature' and the silent acceptance of others – he
becomes dogmatic or mystical about the properties of semen to
prolong the being of the male:

> As you get older, you begin to grow more and more obsessed
> with procreation. You begin to feel used up. Another part of
> oneself is fast diminishing. There isn't that much of oneself
> left. I'm not talking now in any crude sense of how much
> semen there is left in the barrel. I'm saying that one's very
> *being* is being used up.[61]

Given the changing sexual climate in America in the early sixties, Mailer is concerned to differentiate his advocacy of the
sexual revolution from the sexual permissiveness he finds in
American society. But he is not yet able to integrate his concern
for procreation with his other ideas on science and social organisation as he does in *The Prisoner of Sex*.

As the polarities in this thinking generally deepen, his polarisation of men and women, of masculinity and femininity
becomes more and more marked. 'Masculinity' becomes not an
accident of birth for the individual which is reinforced by the
acquisition of certain socially defined characteristics, but a
heroic creation of the individual man. From this definition,
non-masculinity, that is, femininity, becomes defined as non-
heroic, synonymous with lack of courage and strength. Thus,
when in the interview with Paul Krassner in *The Presidential
Papers*, he is asked whether he would endorse Sergius' hostility
to women in the story 'The Time of Her Time', Mailer justifies
the symbolic use of Denise Gondelman in the following terms:

> I would guess that most men who understand women at all,
> feel hostility toward them. At their worst, women are low,
> sloppy beasts.[62]

An attitude which belonged to Croft, Polack and Brown, but

not to the author of *The Naked and the Dead*. Although Mailer goes on to explain that he is also hostile to men and cats, he does not use either of these groups in the same way. When he wishes to condemn the negative qualities of Ban-the-bomb demonstrators, he does not present their failings as part of their being men, but precisely attributes it to their *lack* of 'manliness'.[63] Since manliness and masculinity are increasingly used as images for the qualities Mailer admires, women inevitably suffer from this metaphorical polarisation of the sexes. Writing about the unity of journalism and fiction-writing in *Cannibals and Christians*, he rejects the idealisation of art in the statement that:

Temples are for women.[64]

A conception of art which he has just argued is an inferior one, is appropriately held by women, that is, the inferior half of humanity.

Mailer's ideas on masculinity and femininity, about contraception and procreation, and about sex as a means of absorbing one's partner's 'numa', find their first full fictional expression in *An American Dream*. Whereas in part three of this study I tried to explicate the literary significance of the novel, I want here to examine its implications in terms of the sexual politics involved. These ideas are in fact central to the novel's allegorical structure since it is through the hero's relationship with Deborah, Ruta and Cherry that his progress as a hero is charted, and it is in sexual terms that his experience of almost everything else is imaged. The novel, it seems to me, far more than *The Deer Park*, is 'totally about sex, and totally about morality'. The style bears witness to an almost perfect fusion of Mailer's ideas on sexuality and his ideas on cultural and political life in America. The description of the killing of the four Germans in the Second World War in the first chapter, contains the concepts of choice and salvation, the sexual and religious imagery, the metaphors which shape the significance of the action here and throughout the novel:

Years later I read *Zen in the Art of Archery* and understood the book. Because I did not throw the grenades on that night on the hill under the moon, *it* threw them, and *it* did a near-perfect job. The grenades went off somewhere between five and ten yards over each machine gun, *blast*, *blast*, like boxer's tattoo, one-two, and I was exploded in the butt from a piece of my own shrapnel, whacked with a delicious pain clean as a mistress' sharp teeth going 'Yummy' in your rump, and then the barrel of my carbine swung around like a long fine antenna and pointed itself at the machine-gun hole on my right where a great bloody sweet German face, a healthy spoiled overspoiled young beauty of a face, mother-love all over it making, possessor of that overcurved mouth which only great fat sweet young faggots can have when their rectum is tuned and entertained from adolescence on, came crying, sliding, smiling up over the edge of the hole, 'Hello death!' blood and mud like the herald of sodomy upon his chest, and I pulled the trigger as if I were squeezing the softest breast of the softest pigeon which ever flew, still a woman's breast takes me now and then to the pigeon on that trigger, and the shot cracked like a birth-twig across my palm, *whop*! and the round went in at the base of his nose and spread and I saw his face sucked in backward upon the gouge of the bullet, and he looked suddenly like an old man, toothless, sly, reminiscent of lechery. Then he whimpered *Mutter*, one yelp from the first memory of the womb, and down he went into his own blood just in time, timed like the interval in a shooting gallery, for the next was up, his hole-mate, a hard avenging specter with a pistol in his hand and one arm blown off, rectitude like a stringer of saliva across the straight edge of his lip, the straightest lip I ever saw, German Protestant rectitude.[65]

Rojack is describing the particular way in which he killed the first German in mid-1944, but what the language of the passage really does of course, is to express the *significance* of the event for Rojack's present system of beliefs. It does this, I think, extremely well. Rojack's morality, his beliefs about the interrelationship of violence and sexuality, his association of heterosexuality with health, energy and creativity, and homosexuality with decreative impulses, death and repression, comes through very clearly. Perhaps the best comment on the literary qualities of the passage is that of Richard Poirier in his original review,[66] which is worth quoting at length:

He shows . . . the most intense involvement in the words he uses and in the patterns of association among them. In that long middle sentence there is held in suspension, in a neutralising balance, materials that would in shorter grammatical units – the kind familiar in popular literature of sexual crime – have a psychological luridness which Mailer is choosing here to avoid . . . Given the continuum of movement in that long, unbroken second sentence, none of the implications can be isolated; they are in an interdependent relation that is an image of Rojack's mind. And we are made to feel this even while the simple excitement of what is going on is itself sufficient warrant for the breathlessness of the narrations. Perhaps Mailer planned this sentence, but I suspect it represents something better than planning, some saturation of the author's mind in what he wants to do that makes everything that spontaneously issues from it part of the life that the language has already produced. The fluidity of association is the most frightening aspect of the passage. Thus, though Rojack's dexterity of violence is first ascribed to a sort of magic, it is almost at once re-associated with the vanity of human skill in a sport, boxing, that has a strong component of homoeroticism. From this the mind of the hero quickly shifts to a heterosexual fantasy occasioned by his wound, the comparison being to a woman's affection for his rump, and from there his thoughts move more confidently to the German-soldier-as-faggot, whose 'rectum is tuned.' At this point sodomy gets connected with blood and mud, with death and with something like bodily wastes, and then, from this extremity of explicitness, the drift is back again to a woman and her breast: the act of squeezing the trigger that kills the faggot is like squeezing a breast, the shot itself reminds him of childbirth (it feels like a 'birth twig'), for Rojack the most creative and therefore worthy consequence of heterosexual intercourse. No wonder the cry of the German for 'Mutter' seems dramatically powerful. And it is by the same token metaphorically relevant to the obsessive tension throughout the book between creative sexuality (the German's 'one yelp' is 'from the first memory of the womb') and sex that is murderous, associated with blood, mud, feces and buggery. While the allusion which follows, to the dead soldier's 'hole-mate' (and to his 'rectitude') doesn't require explication, it has the remarkable quality, like everything else in the passage, of being so utterly right in an innocently descriptive way that its metaphoric implications seem natural rather than the result of contrivance.

Poirier's analysis of the passage, and of the book as a whole, is primarily technical; he appreciates it as the powerful dramatisation of a state of mind – which it undoubtedly is. Nevertheless, whilst sharing his admiration for the stylistic achievements of the novel (the review's primary intention was to correct the dismissive attitudes of other critics toward the book's literary qualities), it seems to me important to question the morality being so brilliantly presented. Although the use of image and symbol may indeed be 'utterly right', Rojack's narrow and melodramatic conception of creative sexuality is, I think, at the very least highly questionable.

The same structure of metaphors, and the same values, underlie the descriptions of the hero's sexual activity with Ruta and Cherry, and the scene in which he confronts Kelly. Before these developments however Rojack meets and murders his wife, thus performing the central action of his dream. Her character and her relationship with Rojack (and thus his motive for murder) is presented through the use of symbol and image, not in the realistic analysis of speech and action which Mailer uses for Eitel and Elena's relationship in *The Deer Park*.* The relation between Deborah's destructiveness and Kelly's incestuous use of her is indicated in Rojack's narrative, but not developed. (The presentation of their marriage resembles Lawrence's symbolic use of the moon to present the failure of Ursula and Strebensky's relationship in *Women in Love*, rather than Fitzgerald's treatment of Dick Diver and Nicola Warren's marriage in *Tender is the Night*.) Instead Mailer relies largely on the use of the classical myth of Hecate and an intensive use of olfactory imagery. (The smells and odours which Rojack ident-

* 'She is the centre of the novel's action, the object of Rojack's lengthy speculation, the whole reason, we feel, for the book itself. And she is either lamely generalised, or preposterously unconvincing.' Elizabeth Hardwick, 'Bad Boy', *Partisan Review* (Mar 1965). This is a key example of the comments of critics who, demanding the old stable ego of character and realistic characterisation, failed to respond to Mailer's use of imagery and symbol.

ifies with different characters are of course not indicative of their physical states but symbolic of their mental and moral state.) Deborah is Rojack's Hecate – as Cherry becomes a sort of Magna Dea – as well as the 'Devil's daughter'[67], and her rapport with the moon, her magical powers, the cluster of animal images and her carefully detailed love of hunting establish her in this role. Hecate, who is Persephone in hell, Diana on earth, and Luna in heaven, had powers extending over heaven and hell and earth – hence the relevance of Deborah's family motto: 'Victoria in Caelo Terraque'.[68] The Persephone aspect is suggested in the light-darkness, devil-angel antithesis, a passing reference to the 'robber bridegroom', and the cave-cellar-pit imagery with which the first two chapters are studded. From her death Rojack hopes to inherit her 'light', the qualities she cannot take with her to the underworld:

> I knelt to turn her over. She was bad in death. A beast stared back at me. Her teeth showed, the point of light in her eye was violent, and her mouth was open. It looked like a cave. I could hear some wind which reached down to the cellars of a sunless earth. A little line of spit came from the corner of her mouth, and at an angle from her nose one green seed had floated its small distance on an abortive rill of blood.[69]

Her 'Luna' qualities are even more explicitly maintained, and Rojack's relation to her and his responsibility for her death is developed largely in terms of his subjection to the moon's influence. The moon images persist through his encounters with Ruta and Cherry, through the balcony scene, and into the epilogue where the phone call to Cherry made 'in the moonlight' suggests that he will never be free from the moon's influence – from his responsibility for Deborah's death.

The animal imagery which surrounds her presentation serves to reinforce the classical symbolism but also, especially in the olfactory aspects, to maintain her as the bitch-heiress of popular fiction who deserves in some sense, to be killed:

> We had been married most intimately and often most unhappily for eight years, and for the last five I had been trying to evacuate my expeditionary army, that force of hopes, all-out need, plain virile desire and commitment which I had spent

on her. It was a losing war, and I wanted to withdraw, count my dead, and look for love in another land, but she was a great bitch, Deborah, a lioness of the species: unconditional surrender was her only raw meat. A Great Bitch has losses to calculate after all if the gent gets away.[70]

The 'gent' does succeed in this case, by dint of murdering her, but must work out his strategy for survival with another of her kind, the maid. It is upon Ruta's body that the hero works out the tactics for his next campaign; having obtained a new sense of himself and a 'new grace'[71] by killing his evil spirit, he hopes to learn from her German proletarian maid all that he needs to survive in the world:

> drawing up on the instant out of her a wet spicy wisdom of all the arts and crafts of getting along in the world.[72]

Patterns of imagery similar to those used in the encounter with the German soldiers, are used to evoke the struggle between creative and decreative impulses in the hero's mind. Ruta represents not the forces of evil so much as a field of conflicting forces and desires. She is imaged as a city of choices whose buildings – the mills, graveyards, warehouses, churches and prisons – signify the different options available to Rojack. Since her womb has come to signify responsibility and therefore prison for him, he chooses to ejaculate in her anus, escaping imprisonment but thereby committing himself to the devil:

> ... the seed was expiring in the wrong field ... It was perishing in the kitchens of the Devil. Was its curse on me?
> 'Der Teufel is so happy,' she said, and a perfect spitefulness of attention came to a focus in her eyes.[73]

When later that night Rojack reverses his commitment and chooses to send his 'seed' into the right field of Cherry's womb, he symbolically takes a step towards God and creation. The episodes with Cherry are described not in animal and olfactory imagery, but in the 'positive' images of sea and sun; her blondeness, her 'wheat-coloured wrapper' and her eyes which are 'golden with light' associate her with creativity and fertility. And when Rojack removes the 'corporate rubbery obstruction' which he detests so much, and dissolves her will which has been 'like a girdle of steel about her womb', she emerges renewed, as a fit mate for the hero:

> in her sleep a sweet blonde girl of seventeen smiled back at me, skin almost luminous, a golden child, pure Georgia peach, a cheer leader, sweet fruit, national creation.[74]

Mailer uses the women characters as secondary human beings who are indices of his hero's moral development and who do not have any autonomous moral character themselves; but then, apart from Rojack all the characters in the novel, both male and female, exist primarily as symbolic, essentialist creations – Kelly and Shago Martin as much as Deborah, Ruta and Cherry. But with the three women characters in particular, he uses the sentimental clichéd imagery of the popular crime-thriller where women are 'sweet blondes', 'Great Bitches', 'alley-cat' foreign maids or merely 'very silly little girls'. In this sense Rojack's women are indeed 'national creations' since they are based on the male American myths about women and sexuality which feed the 'hordes of the mediocre and the mad'. But since Rojack is presented also as an intellectual capable of criticising the national myths, the object presumably is not to show him in the clutch of such popular conceptions, but to exploit the clichéd simplicities of pop-fiction categories on the way to other significances, as Poirier puts it. To write, that is, a moral allegory of an existential kind. Mailer apparently sees no contradiction between basing his hero's existentialist 'morality' on the reduced, distorted conceptions of women found in popular fiction and this is, in my opinion, a fundamental failure of judgement – Mailer's failure, not merely Rojack's, since the author clearly presents his hero's beliefs as heroic if not strictly possible. He does of course acknowledge the private nature of Rojack's vision in the title and perhaps in the ending of the story; but although his existential logic is *viable* only in the hipster's 'dream', it is valid generally, Mailer suggests, in its implications. Rojack's thesis about the absolute value of acting out his instincts (to the point of murder, anal rape, the brutal beating of one's ideological opponents, etc.) is only a dream, but within the novel it is a positive dream – a dream of health in fact. The celebration of creative, fertile sexuality takes place in terms which are morally affirmative, but which also imply the

total subjugation of women to this 'creative' sexuality, the rigid
elimination of other forms of sexuality and sexual ideology. In
short, there is a celebration (in the action and in the language)
of violence and repression in the name of a single form of
'health'. And this I think must be considered not merely as an
extra-literary, moral or ideological criticism (which has its own
validity) but also as an important artistic flaw. To make his
allegorical scheme, his images and symbols depend on a neo-
primitivist sexual ideology (which, while one can see the logic of
it in the novel, requires a lengthy explication and justification
outside the scope of a short allegorical novel), seems to me a
major artistic limitation. Mailer has based one of his richest
and highly organised stylistical novels on a highly questionable
private philosophical system. He draws on every kind of
mythic, religious reference, and on metaphors taken from every
level of existence to convey his hero's state of mind and values,
yet behind the brilliant and elaborate surface of the language,
Rojack and his author's attitudes appear to me to be bigoted,
histrionic and reactionary.

The Prisoner of Sex constitutes a defence and a development of
the attitudes which appear not merely in *An American Dream* but
also in *Why are We in Vietnam?* and *A Fire on the Moon*. Some of the
best sections of this book fall outside, or rather between, the
main arguments about the relations between the sexes; the
opening chapter of 'The Prizewinner' which recalls the tone
and technique of *The Armies of the Night*, the vignette on the
summer in Maine, the short story within 'The Advocate' where
Mailer imagines Lawrence's struggle with homosexuality. But
although he repeatedly promises to confront his thinking on
women, to come to terms with the radical elements in
Women's Liberation 'which could not be ignored unless he
were to cease thinking of himself as a revolutionary',[75] the overwhelming evidence of the book points to the total lack of original writing and thinking. The appreciation of the style of some
of the new women writers, the shock of recognising the radicalism in Women's Liberation, the final admission that women
may have the right to more than a good 'mate' and children,
are minor concessions beside the running arguments. The
argument is in fact an extension of the ideas on science and
social organisation found in his previous work: that in so far as

Women's Liberation is based on certain technological advances, on forces which interfere with the natural and 'heroic'
state between the sexes, they are part of the totalitarianism of
modern life:

> he had not set out to collect the most entertaining exhibits of
> a new intellectual fashion but rather to explore the revol-
> utionary ideas which emerged from these collective pam-
> phlets, books, and bible of Women's Lib, and explore them
> with all awareness that they were twentieth century ideas,
> and so might be artfully designed to advance the fortunes of
> the oncoming technology of the state. What a paranoid sup-
> position was this! Yet how reasonable. Paranoia and
> common sense come together as the world goes insane.[76]

Mailer, as the Prizewinner or the Prisoner of Wedlock, again
assumes the role of the embattled writer, defender of the faith:
faith in a God-given order of instincts and vision. In this stance
the only question he raises is in fact whether the developments
in the sexual field are 'the beginning of the technologising of sex
or a call from the deep'.[77] He acknowledges as much in his argument and in his imagery, conceiving of the 'primal war' between the sexes as another campaign in the larger war which he
has been waging for the last twenty years. Picking his way
through the arguments of the vaginal *vs* the clitoral orgasm, he
feels the loss of old assumptions about vaginal orgasm to be
equivalent to a major military defeat –

> – he had a glimpse of how Tories reacted when India was
> lost.[78]

Whilst aligning himself, without misgivings, with social reactionaries of previous eras, Mailer the unregenerate revolutionary is less happy with the parallels between his arguments
and those of twentieth-century conservatives. Quoting at
length a passage from Hitler on the question of women, he
denies the disturbing aspects of the comparison by arguing that
the Nazi propaganda about vision and instincts was essentially
a cover for their real commitment to the machine and a technological state. He further suggests that:

– one could even argue that the Nazis had been the diabolical success of a Devil who wished to cut man off from his primitive instincts and thereby leave us marooned in a plastic maze which could shatter the balance of nature before the warnings were read.[79]

Mailer thus attempts to justify his sexual conservatism, his willingness to resume arguments discredited by the Nazis' use of them, as a heroic defence against the Devil and the 'plastic maze'. Ironically, in dismissing twentieth-century liberalism and technological advance as the unwitting tools of the Devil, and by raising his standard as the champion of radical instincts, he makes (for a 'revolutionary') a classically conservative gesture: the claim that in fact 'God is on his side.'

After defending with some skill his fellow generals, Miller and Lawrence, from the 'sawn-off shotgun'[80] of Kate Millett, he goes on to affirm his own conception of the roles of men and women. He does this in terms of his mystical biology and his existential view of time. Man exists in the present, and his sexual force is not an accident of birth or a socially defined attribute but 'the adventurous juncture of ego and courage . . . his finest moral product'.[81] Women because of their childbearing capacities, exist 'beyond' the present, have a grasp on the future which is their real consolation for the limitations of being a woman in the present:

> how could a woman compete if she contained the future as well as the present and so lived a physical life on the edge of the divide?[82]

His argument about the advantages of being a woman are a parody of the religious ideas about being deprived on earth, but richly rewarded in heaven – the language in which he expresses these ideas is certainly full of borrowed biblicisms. He uses a mixture of both religious and existentialist ideas to ballast his argument, but his real support is primitivism, the god of phallicism, Priapus, whom he 'quotes' in the following way:

> perhaps a cunt, smelly though it may be, is one of the prime symbols for the connection between all things.[83]

Beyond the rhetoric of *The Prisoner of Sex*, the verbal and imaginative play, lies a contradictory argument and an impoverished view of the sexes as human beings. Having stated that women 'possess the better half of life already'[84] but also that as a 'privileged element of nature'[85] they do not need liberating into the responsibilities and burdens of men, he can only reiterate his separate-but-equal policy, a tarted-up version of his statement in *The Presidential Papers*:

> Was it too late now to suggest that in the search for the best mate was concealed the bravery of a woman, for to find the best mate (whatever ugly or brutal or tyrannical or unbalanced or heart-searing son of misery he might appear) was no easy matter but indeed a profound and artistic search for that mysterious fellow of concealed values who would eventually present himself in those twenty-three most special chromosomes able to cut through fashion, tradition and class.[86]

Should this inducement fail to convince, there are histrionic warnings about the consequences which will follow women's refusal of 'the profound and artistic search for that mysterious fellow'. (At such points as these the 'PW' looks like the reactionary fear-ridden patriarch he has been painted.) But despite the pseudo-scientific disquisitions on chromosomes, and the heavy artillery rhetoric, there is little 'masculine' rationality to show *why* Mailer divides the world as he does:

> between artists and engineers, prophets and programmers, adventurers and technicians, guerrillas and organised echelons of the nonviolent . . .[87]

He makes it quite clear though where he places 'commissar' Millett and Women's Liberation writers with their 'prose reminiscent of the worst of the old party line'.[88] They belong (despite the veiled hope of a messiah on the last page) with the hacks occupying History's seat, with the bureaucrats and technicians, the genetic engineers as opposed to the artists, prophets and adventurers. Reproducing once more his hip-square oppositions in another guise, Mailer reduces all new experience, all the complexity of the new ideas about women into fodder for his old dichotomies. In *The Prisoner of Sex*, Mailer has, it seems to me, written himself into an intellectual and stylistic blind alley.

Conclusion

Mailer has taken an increasingly active role with regard to his own work, not merely in becoming the 'hero' of his later books, but as a critic and commentator on his own literary career. In the late forties and early fifties, he produced several articles for the magazine *Dissent* and his first three novels, but remained for the most part silent about the process of their production, about his problems, self-assessment and general views on literature. His view of literary work as a vocation changed, as I have suggested in the third part of this study, as the result of his experience of writing and publishing *The Deer Park*, and this change was fully documented in *Advertisements for Myself*. His conception of himself as a 'psychic outlaw'[1] and of life as a battle whose characteristic attitude was hostility, began with this crucial personal and literary experience:

> And so as the language of sentiment would have it, something broke in me, but I do not know if it was so much a loving heart, as a cyst on the weak, the unreal, and the needy, and I was finally open to my anger. I turned within my psyche I can almost believe, for I felt something shift to murder in me. I finally had the simple sense to understand that if I wanted my work to travel further than others, the life of my talent depended on fighting a little more . . .[2]

Ideas about struggle, conflict and violence had of course figured prominently in the situations and imagery of his early work. *The Naked and the Dead* was a war story of which the central theme was, in his own words, 'the conflict between the beast and the seer'. His second novel uses the cold-war period in American politics as its setting, and ends with its hero taking up the struggle against barbarianism armed with the 'little

160

object'. In his third novel, the three heroes continue to battle, with one capitulating to forces stronger than himself, another imprisoned by a hostile and stronger world, and only the writer, Sergius O'Shaughnessy, free to use his art to 'blow against the walls of every power that exists'.[3]

The specific oppositions and conflicts of Mailer's imagination amalgamate in his fourth book into a conception of the world in which war is the prevailing condition not merely for his fictional creations but for the writer himself – and even for God. It is in the 'hipsters' section of *Advertisements for Myself* that Mailer first formulates his conception of an existential God who exists 'as a warring element in a divided universe'[4] and of men as the embodiments of that God's 'embattled vision'.[5] In the following years this conception of existence is never absent from his world, and within it Mailer develops his most central ideas about writing. He uses his intellectual energies to absorb and transform a whole range of ideas into material for this battle, while his imaginative powers are, it seems to me, pressed into the service of this 'war'. Although practically everything he has written since is marred by this 'embattled vision', his work is inconceivable without it. It becomes the central contradiction in his development, and his three most considerable books since *The Naked and the Dead* – *Advertisements for Myself*, *An American Dream*, and *The Armies of the Night* – are based on this conception of himself and the world.

Many of the images of his later work and the reference to the Texan Cavalry in *The Armies of the Night* and *A Fire on the Moon* recall the combat situations in *The Naked and the Dead* and some critics, notably Robert Bone,[6] have suggested that Mailer's aggressiveness, his view of the artist as a 'squad leader' are the product of his own experience of combat in World War II. Kate Millett has attempted to trace the origin of Mailer's sexual attitudes back to the same source, to the 'men's-house culture of the army'.[7] This seems to me an over-simplification; for while he has undoubtedly drawn many of his attitudes and images from this experience, the embattled stance has a more direct literary significance. In *Cannibals and Christians*, in the play interview already discussed, Mailer defined 'form in general' as 'the record of a war' and explains his view of a writer's style as the 'detailed record of an engagement'.[8] Although the mystical strain of his exposition makes it difficult to gauge exactly what he means by war in this instance, it is clear that he has come to regard 'war' as an appropriate metaphor for writing in general, and for his own work in particular. His writing, his use of language and imagery is intended not merely to describe the conflicts in the 'divided universe' but to be a weapon in the struggle. Or, as he expresses it at the end of the Paris interview in the same volume:

> . . . it's no little matter to be a writer. There's that godawful 'Time' Magazine world out there, and one can make raids on it. There are palaces and prisons to attack. One can even succeed now and again in blowing holes in the line of the world's communications. Sometimes I feel as if there's a vast guerrilla war going on for the mind of man, communist against communist, capitalist against capitalist, artist against artist.[9]

Mailer's involvement in this 'vast guerrilla war' has been what enabled him to continue writing at a critical point in his writing career, and he has used it as the scaffolding of his best subsequent work. It liberated him in effect from the influences and borrowings of the previous literary generation, and from a narrow 'literary' approach to subject matter and style. But his 'warlike' conception of himself and the world now seems to me as constricting as it was once liberating. His desire to 'have his hand on the rump of History',[10] to use his writing in a direct interventionist way on current social and cultural affairs, has become self-defeating. For although works of the imagination can exert great political and social influence, they do so, I think, in very complex and long-term ways – achieving effects which Mailer's writing about the space programme and Women's Liberation are unlikely to do. And although he has shown some dissatisfaction with his recent achievements, Mailer has not yet abandoned his self-imposed burden of 'making a revolution in the consciousness of our time' nor the conception of writing as a 'war' or as a weapon. Even his most perceptive and sympathetic critics, whilst they have identified the crisis in his present work, have failed to challenge him on this fundamental issue – his confusion of the role of the artist and propagandist.

To compare a work of imagination with a weapon in a war, as Mailer explicitly or implicitly is continually doing, is to resort to a dangerous and misleading metaphor. It seems to me particularly dangerous for a writer whose gifts lie primarily in his creative abilities with language rather than in his naively systematising kind of intelligence, and his neo-primitivist world view. The metaphor is misleading for reasons which John Berger has suggested in another context, in a recent article on art as propaganda:

> The effectiveness of a weapon can be estimated quantitatively. Its performance is isolatable and repeatable. One chooses a weapon for a situation. The effectiveness of a work of imagination cannot be estimated quantitatively. Its performance is not isolatable or repeatable. It changes with circumstances. It creates its own situation. There is no *foreseeable* quantitative correlation between the quality of a work and its effectiveness. And this is part of its nature because it is intended to operate within a field of subjective interactions which are interminable and immeasurable. This is not to grant to art an ineffable value; it is only to emphasise that the imagination, when true to its impulses, is continually and inevitably questioning the existing category of usefulness.[11]

In his work, Mailer has of course continually questioned the 'existing categories of usefulness', by challenging the imperatives of an advanced technological society and by dealing in his writing with areas of the imagination and experience usually ignored or excluded by other contemporary writers. But both *A Fire on the Moon* and *The Prisoner of Sex* show a desperate and unquestioning loyalty to the vision which served him earlier and which he is still affirming:

> But he knew that no matter how conservative he became, nor how much he began to believe that the marrows and sinews of creation were locked in the roots of the amputated past, he was still a revolutionary, for conservatism had been destroyed by the corporations of the conservatives, their plastic, their advertising, their technology.[12]

The style and statements of this last book suggest that Mailer has become 'locked' not merely in an anachronistic and utopian radicalism, but that he is in danger of becoming locked in his own 'amputated past' and becoming, like his own literary hero, Hemingway, parasitic on his earlier achievements. For, despite his profound sense of current history and his significant contributions to literature and radicalism, his work stands in need, as Richard Poirier has commented, of 'some larger redemptive effort',[13] if he is to become more than a talented and interesting minor writer. To escape this 'fate', it seems to me – on the evidence of his own work – vital that he control his impatient desire to make 'History' and accept the more long-term perspectives of writing literature.

Epilogue

In the last three years Mailer has produced three new books*
and he is shortly to publish another, *The Faith of Graffiti*. His two
previous books, *A Fire on the Moon* and *The Prisoner of Sex*, were
disappointing, I argued, because he used the space programme
and women's liberation as grist for his old satanic mills – the
system of dualisms which has dominated his work since the
mid-fifties. The writer who in *The Armies of the Night* prides himself on changing his style according to his project, who values
'openness' to new experience and ideas above consistency,
seemed then in real danger of self-parody. Readers, critics and
Mailer himself feared that his particular literary talents were
being diverted into a journalistic war against the technologising
of America.

His three latest productions do little to allay that fear. *St.
George and the Godfather* is a report on the 1972 American political
conventions, *Existential Errands* another collection of essays, and
Marilyn his first biography. None of them, in other words, is the
long awaited 'big novel' that Mailer has been promising to
write for so long now. Although different from each other in
genre, as regards philosophy and style, all three are continuous
with his previous work. And although 'King of the Hill', which
is reprinted in *Existential Errands*, provides evidence of the fact
that Mailer still possesses enormous abilities as an imaginative
writer, none of these three books represents a full expression of
those abilities. But whether as reporter, essayist, polemicist or
biographer Mailer still relates to the world primarily as a writer
– through the structures of language in which he reflects and
struggles to transform contemporary reality. Neither his films,

* *St. George and the Godfather* (Sep 1972); *Existential Errands* (Apr 1973); *Marilyn*,
(1973).

165

nor his activities as a public figure or political candidate, alter this essential fact. Perhaps the chief importance of this latest work is the way in which it illuminates Mailer's problems – aesthetic, social and personal – as a writer in contemporary America. Why the 'novelistic impulse' is continually diverted into other forms, is the specific question which Mailer raises but does not resolve here.

In *St. George and the Godfather* he writes about the Democratic and Republican conventions of 1972, again assuming the persona of 'the modest and half-invisible Aquarius'.[1] Having stated that he finds it incredible,

> how people could keep studying the minutiae of a convention on a television set for hours when the greatest part of those details had to be incomprehensible to them, or at next to void of connotation, low in entertainment value and usually boring . . .[2]

he proceeds to give a full-length prose study of those minutiae. In a different medium the message is also different. The approach is that used for the 1964 and 1968 conventions: the differences between Republicans and Democrats are used to represent the gulf between the two halves of the schizophrenic nation, while the gap between party policy and political reality he ascribes to totalitarianism. Not merely do the old preoccupations underlie his reportage, but the voice of the 'modest and half-invisible' Aquarius continually echoes and sometimes directly quotes from Mailer's past pronouncements. Politically, too, there are few changes of position.

Particular attention is given to American involvement in Southeast Asia, as in Mailer's previous political writing. The policy of the Johnson administration is compared with that of Nixon's government, and the withdrawal from Vietnam is contrasted with increased American activity in Laos and Cambodia. Using fictionalised dialogue between politicians, newspaper reports, psychological explanations involving Satan and Jehovah, a 'diary-entry' of a Vietnamese child, together with carefully substantiated figures and bombing statistics from the 'Congressional Record', Mailer orchestrates his massive indictment of American foreign policy. Passages of political rhetoric within this running argument are extremely effective:

One hundred seventy-six thousand tons of bombs had been dropped on Cambodia in the last two years, and that was more than all the bombs dropped on Japan in World War II. Cambodia! Our ally! but on Laos it was not 176,000 tons but more than a million. We had in fact dropped more bombs altogether in the three and a half years of Nixon's reign than we dropped on Europe and Asia in World War II, indeed almost twice as many bombs and there was no industry, military population, railroad yards, or any other category of respectable target to compare with Germany, Italy and Japan, no, finally not much more than the wet earth, the dirt roads, the villages, the packing-crate cities and the people – so the bombing had become an activity as rational as the act of a man who walks across his own home town to defecate each night on the lawn of a stranger – it is the same stranger each night – such a man could not last long even if he had the most powerful body in town. 'Stop', he would scream as they dragged him away, 'I need to shit on that lawn. Its the only way to keep my body in shape, you fools. A bat has bitten me!'[3]

Clearly, Mailer finds in America's Asian wars an objective correlative for the madness he sees loose in American life, and he manages to make the point humorously, without detracting from the seriousness of the wars.

On women, he uses the same arguments and images he used in *The Prisoner of Sex*. Writing about the abortion and contraception plank in the Democratic Party platform, and how it was abandoned during the convention, he briefly restates his position. Rejecting the idea of the specific oppression of women, he cannot accept the parallel of sexism with racism:

they pretended to a suffering as profound as the Blacks, when their anguish came out of nothing more intolerable than the intolerable pointlessness of middle-class life.[4]

While claiming to have always supported the legal right to abortion, he remains opposed to contraception, particularly the use of the pill, which he says removes the 'dignity' of a nightly choice not to conceive. He continues to associate the

women's liberation movement with the forces of totalitarianism, and again his hatred of technology and his organic conception of womanhood lie behind this attitude. The domination of
a woman's 'will' over her instincts, or natural functions, is seen
as inherently destructive:

> . . . at the bottom of Women's Liberation was all the ex
> plosive of alienated will, a will now so detached from any of
> the old female functions, and hence so autocratic that
> insanity, cancer, or suicidal collapse might have to be the
> penalty . . .[5]

When this statement is compared with the celebration of 'will'
in the male boxers in 'King of the Hill', it is obvious that Mailer
is still using his double standard: an existentialist conception of
men, and an essentialist conception of women.

One of the strengths of *St. George and the Godfather* is the emphasis on the fact that the events of the conventions take place
within a complicated system of mass-communications. His perception that the media 'make history as well as report it'[6], while
not of course original, is nevertheless a fundamentally important one. The view of party conventions as pageant-politics was
present in his earlier political essays but here it is developed
further. Conventions are seen as 'shows' directed by party
bureaucrats for television networks, and politicians as the products of a public relations-media system as powerful as any
studio star system. Mailer suggests fairly pointedly that the
political fate of Senator Eagleton, for example, was largely determined by the press and television networks. Apart from Eagleton and the reference to the fairytale in the title, the role of the
media is discussed most forcefully in relation to the Republicans, in Section 3, suggestively entitled 'Program'. After
making the McLuhanish statement that 'the communication
itself would be the convention,'[7] Mailer expands his point
through a series of metaphors and images. The 'Nixon Spectacular' is described as an 'epic' with a technically impressive
set designed to resemble 'the bastions of a castle and the battlements of a medieval fort'.[8] The hero of this epic is of course
Nixon, the Godfather, with his wife and 'starlet' daughters in
supporting roles. Nixon is not just the leading man but also a
director, an 'Eisenstein of the mediocre' who co-ordinates the

whole show. Although Mailer dislikes the 'script', he finds it a successful production for the American public. Like so many Mailer villains, Nixon is presented as a good communications engineer who is able to incorporate the anti-Republican demonstrators camped in Flamingo Park into the program. Thus the Yippies become 'extras' and their symbolic protests are converted into entertainment by the television cameras:

> The occasional insertion of the street action, however, didn't hurt; in fact, it helped to spark the product which emerged as a species of new TV film (in effect!) as sophisticated in its mass wad-like way as a work by Jean Luc Godard . . .[9]

About his own role in this communications network, Mailer is less clear cut. At one point he compares himself to an anthropologist, a neutral note-taker whose descriptions are,

> analogous perhaps to the kind of notes anthropologists might take on the comings and goings of baboons in the brush.[10]

But Aquarius, prophet-moralist as well as reporter, really attempts to provide an alternative to the television coverage, an anti-heroic reading of the events and personalities he observes. He does this through detailed observations on faces, voices, clothes and manners, seizing the psychological and sociological nuances, and placing characters, often very astutely, in the American social scene. There are some excellent vignettes, as good as the famous characterisation of the Goldwater supporters of 1964. One of the best of these is his portrait of Spiro Agnew at a press conference held in Vizcaya Palace on the coast near Miami. The passage imitates the movement of a camera, first presenting Agnew as a figure in the middle distance, in a dark suit and white shirt, 'composed and remote' amid some marble busts, and then panning sideways to focus on the visual details of his surroundings: the nymphs and gargoyles of grey coral, the combo and black waiters serving drinks on the terrace, the buffet under a pink tent, the white chairs and tables with their ornate patterns of holes which repeat the 'much-pocked look' of the walls and coral, and give the impression that 'all Vizcaya has been spattered with bullets'. And with this metaphor, character and surroundings are suddenly brought into relation, the camera zooms in, as it were, for the close-up and with it, Mailer's rhetorical epiphany:

> . . . the steel shutters cranked up high on the arches of the loggia, Agnew's suit assumes its focus. He looks, of course! he looks like he is wearing just the suit a Latin American dictator would wear in his palace by the tropical sea, and indeed has there ever been a man as high in American public life who has looked this much like the general who throws over a banana republic in a putsch?[11]

There are other good portraits of individuals – Wallace, McGovern, Pat Nixon – and of groups like the Young Voters For the President, and the Yippies in Flamingo Park 'smelling the pot which dissipates as slowly as the odor of honeysuckle'.[12] The style of the book, though sometimes strained and repetitive, is generally good. As intelligent, humorous and perceptive reportage of contemporary events, it recalls Lowell's praise of Mailer as 'the best journalist in America' (which was followed by Mailer's retort that there were days 'when I think of myself as being the best writer in America').[13] Nevertheless, despite the passages of imaginative writing, and the echoes of Villon and Blake, *St. George* is very definitely 'journalism', that is, writing which is intended to have an effect *today*, here and now, and prepared to sacrifice other, more long-term effects on the imagination, to achieve this. So that, inevitably, when the events it deals with are absorbed into what Mailer calls 'the seizure of history', the book will lose a great deal, if not all, of its significance.

Mailer raises this question himself in the preface of his next book, *Existential Errands*. Introducing the collection of letters, speeches, reviews and articles written between 1966 and 1971, he writes of the choice between 'a certain big novel' and the 'moot desire to have one's immediate say on contemporary matters (which) kept diverting the novelistic impulse into journalism'.[14] This statement is doubly interesting for students of Mailer's work. First, he makes a distinction between journalism and art (the 'big novel') which in the conversation with Robert Lowell in *The Armies of the Night* he implicitly rejects, subsuming both activities under the term 'writer'. Secondly, when Mailer began his non-fictional writing in *Advertisements For Myself,* he described his objectives as 'making a revolution in the consciousness of our time', but here he speaks of 'having one's say on contemporary matters'. The more prosaic formulation suggests that he is beginning to recognise the limitations of journalism, to see it as a diversion from his real impulse. This recognition is certainly relevant to what follows. The 'novelistic impulse' in *Existential Errands* is given full expression only in 'King of the Hill', and the rest of the book – Mailer having his immediate say – is undeniably inferior.

'King of the Hill', the essay on Mohhamed Ali, is by far the best piece of writing in the collection. In its stylistic concentration it invites comparison not so much with 'Death' – his essay on the Patterson-Liston fight in *The Presidential Papers* – but with the expedition sections of *The Naked and the Dead* or the passages on the killing of the Germans in *An American Dream.* Although the characters, Ali, Liston and Frazier, are of course well-known American figures, and the climax (the outcome of the Ali-Frazier fight) predetermined, 'King of the Hill' is organised like a short-story around plot, suspense, tightly controlled patterns of imagery and a poetic exploitation of language. The hero, Mohammed Ali, is first introduced and his representative significance suggested as 'America's Greatest Ego' in an ego-dominated society. The second scene describes the heavyweight boxing world and the Ali-Liston fights, thus preparing the way for the Ali-Frazier fight which forms the crisis of the essay-story. Scene 3 presents Ali in training, emphasising his skill as an artist, a boxer who can make trainers 'weep openly' in the workouts. Frazier is then shown in training, as an equally monumental but less verbal ego, whose qualities of discipline and strength are the counterpart of Ali's artistry. The fifth part of the essay takes us to the ring, from the afternoon weigh-in to the fifth round of the fight; then, in the last pages, Mailer describes round by round, point by point, the battle between the two giants which ends with Frazier's heroic win and Ali's equally heroic defeat.

Throughout the twenty-eight page essay, the pace is brilliantly controlled, the action well dramatised, and all supplementary information perfectly lodged within the line of narrative. Mailer's view of boxing as an 'existential venture'

and his related view of boxers as 'prodigies of will'[15] is expressed
in his characterisation of Frazier and Ali; their physical qualities – energy and stamina – are celebrated and given a moral
dimension. They emerge not merely as national heroes, cham-
pions in the world of sport, but as the literary descendants of
Croft, the fifties hipsters and the Mailer creations of the late sixties:

> What separates the noble ego of the prizefighters from the
> lesser ego of authors is that the fighter goes through experi-
> ences in the ring which are occasionally immense, incom-
> municable except to fighters who have been as good . . .
> Like men who climb mountains it is an exercise of ego
> which becomes something like soul . . .[16]

The parallel between fighters and authors and the mountain-climber simile establishes the heroic identification. Mailer
then goes on to emphasise, in imagery strongly reminiscent of
The Naked and the Dead, that the energy, 'risk' and will-power
found in the ring are the existential experiences of the twentieth
century.

> So, two great fighters in a great fight travel down subter-
> ranean rivers of exhaustion and cross mountain peaks of
> agony, stare at the light of their own death in the eye of the
> man they are fighting, travel into the crossroads of the
> most excruciating choice of karma as they get up from the
> floor against all the appeal of the sweet swooning cata-
> combs of oblivion . . .[17]

In the 'Death' article of 1963 Mailer's views on boxing
(quoted above) stand out as unacceptable assertions – a jarring
'voice-over' the scenes in the ring. Here those views are fully
integrated in the style of the essay, the 'language of the body' is
captured in the rhythms, syntax and imagery of the prose. Thus
the balletic speed and variety of Ali's style is conveyed in the
quick succession of similes, in a long sentence divided into
short, rhythmic units:

> . . . he played with punches, was tender with them, laid
> them on as delicately as you would put a postage stamp on
> an envelope, then cracked them in like a riding crop across

your face, stuck a cruel jab like a baseball bat held head on
into your mouth, next waltzed you into a clinch with a
tender arm around your neck, winged away out of reach on
flying legs, dug a hook with a full swing of a baseball bat
hard into your ribs, hard pokes of a jab into the face, a
mocking flurry of pillows and gloves, a mean forearm cutting you off from coming up on him, a cruel wrestling of
your neck in a clinch, then elusive again, gloves snake-
licking your face like a whip.[18]

For the heavier, more powerful boxing style of Frazier, he uses
mechanical imagery with long syntactical structures punctu-
ated by groups of sound-words. The sounds of words are exploited to the full; assonance, alliteration and onomatopoeia
are combined, as deliberately as in a poem by Tennyson, to re-
produce not simply the extreme sensations of the boxers, but
also to direct the reader's response toward the significance of
the experience:

Frazier went on with the doggedness, the concentration,
the pumped-up fury of a man who has had so little in his
life that he can endure torments to get everything, he
pushed the total of his energy and force into an absolute
exercise of will so it did not matter if he fought a sparring
partner or the heavy bag, he lunged at each equally as if
the exhaustions of his own heart and the clangor of his
lungs were his only enemies, and the head of a fighter or
the leather of the bag as it rolled against his own head was
nothing but some abstract thunk of material, not a thing,
not a man, but thunk! thunk! thunk! something of an
obstacle, thunk! thunk! thunk! to beat into thunk! obliv-
ion. And his breath came in rips and sobs as he smashed
into the bag as though it were real, just that heavy big
torso-sized bag hanging from its chain – but he attacked it
as if it were a bear, as if it were a great fighter and they were
in the mortal embrace of a killing set of exchanges of
punches in the middle of the eighth round, and rounds of
exercise later, skipping rope to an inhumanly fast beat for
this late round in the training day, sweat pouring like jets
of blood from an artery, he kept swinging his rope, mutter-
ing, 'Two-million-dollars-and-change, two-million-

dollars-and-change', railroad train chugging into the ter-
minals of exhaustion.[19]

Like his 'creator' Frazier is a puritan not a hedonist; life is a
struggle and the struggle is not just for two million dollars but
'to get everything'. Clearly this passage is not just a celebration
of the individual boxer, Frazier. Even without the earlier identification of boxer with artist and mountain-climber, the style
signals that this battle has a more general significance. It is an
extended image of heroism, of the 'awfulness' (in the religious
sense) of man's nature and his ability to fight and endure –
whether the enemy be a leather bag, a man, a bear, or his own
physical limitations. Behind this affirmation lies Mailer's view
of life as a constant battle where only by the 'absolute exercise
of will' can man find 'something like soul'.

'King of the Hill', written in 1971, is then a re-affirmation of
one of Mailer's oldest ideas, an idea embryonic in his first three
novels, explicitly stated in subsequent essays and given its apotheosis in *An American Dream*. The romantic rather than existential positive in all his work is this triumphant assertion of the
individual will against all odds and all comers. In *An American
Dream*, Rojack embodied this principle and pitted himself
against the technologised, psychoanalysed life of middle-class
America. Frazier and Mohammed Ali, and the bull-fighter,
Ramirez, in 'Homage to El Loco', embody the same principle.
What they are up against, outside the ring, is dealt with in the
remaining sections of *Existential Errands*.

Few of these pieces have sufficient intrinsic merit to justify
reprinting – almost all of them have appeared in magazines and
newspapers which are still easily available. The first four, in
Part I, on boxing, bull-fighting, theatre and film stand as independent essays, and the long review of Norman Podhoretz's
book *Making It* which opens Part II, contains some interesting
comments on the book and its reception by the American literary 'Establishment'. But the prefaces, interviews, letters and
mayoralty speeches which make up the rest of the collection are
interesting only as contributions to the long, unfinished quasi-
autobiography which began with *Advertisement For Myself*. *Existential Errands* as a collection lacks the overall design but also the
vitality of *Advertisements* and betrays the same intellectual and

stylistic defects which mark *The Presidential Papers* and *Cannibals and Christians*. In the Preface, Mailer concedes that it will mainly interest those already 'sufficiently intrigued with my ideas to try a few more', but the ideas are essentially the same ones and the keenest interest in them is dulled by the end of the 300-odd pages. Occasional insights are lost in the over-extended presentation, and the style is sometimes pompous and often simply verbose. The 'embattled vision' comes to life only in frantic local movements in the prose, a witty use of ob-scenity, the occasional new image. The reader is ceremoniously conducted over the now familiar terrain – technology, smog, plastic foods, Black Power, and sex – which is Mailer's Amer-ica. Landmarks are formally, even perfunctorily, indicated by the writer and there is a distinct sense that Mailer himself is bored with his routines.

In the essay on film he returns to the 'professional' theme which dominated the essays of *The Presidential Papers* to talk about acting and directing problems during the filming of *Maidstone*. He contrasts 'existential' acting with 'professional' acting and defines the latter in terms of ceremony:

> Ceremony is designed, you can say, to mollify the gods, to safeguard us from existential situations precisely because ceremony is repetition.[20]

In these carefully defined terms, his intellectual routines of dis-cussing everything in terms of God and the Devil, technology and instincts, now insulate him from the complexities of con-temporary life, or what he calls 'existential situations'. The combative stance and jargon-infested rhetoric of large parts of *Existential Errands* are not attempts to revolutionise anybody's consciousness, but the instant prose of the professional journalist.

Marilyn published later the same year, is Mailer's first bi-ography. After writing novels, poems, plays, essays and a 'His-tory as Novel', he crosses yet another generic frontier into one of the oldest of literary genres. As a full-length attempt to fictiona-lise non-fictional material, *Marilyn* most resembles *The Armies of the Night*. In the first chapter, 'A Novel Biography', the writer describes how he came to accept the assignment, makes ac-knowledgment of the Zolotow and Guiles biographies, and defines the scope of his own book. Unwilling to write a short, conventional preface to the photographic study, or to attempt a real 'psychohistory' because of the research involved, he expanded the original 25,000 word preface into a 90,000 word 'novel':

> . . . a long biographical article – nonetheless, a *species* of novel ready to play by the rules of biography . . . with the sanction of a novelist . . . to look into the unspoken impulses of some of his real characters.[21]

The new candidate for biographer discusses the 'biographical' problems of the enterprise: the interpretation of different existing accounts, friends' reminiscences, interviews, letters, the factitious nature of newspaper 'factoids' and the unreliability of the subject's own statements. In the same chapter the novelist introduces his principal themes: the dream life of the nation, the roots of insanity, the mystery and uniqueness of the individual.

As material, the life of this particular American actress lends itself almost too easily to Mailer's imaginative patterning. In the portrait of Lulu Meyers, and Cherry in *An American Dream*, Mailer had already drawn on the myth of the beautiful blonde, the 'sweet angel of sex' of which Marilyn Monroe was the supreme example in the fifties. The facts of her life provide him with another opportunity to speculate about women and sexuality, schizophrenia and suicide. Then, as a cultural historian, the fifties and early sixties are his special period, while the role of Hollywood and the creation of national myths is one of the central concerns of his work. The string of people who created Marilyn Monroe out of Norma Jean Baker are different versions of the Supreme Pictures characters in *The Deer Park* – naturally, since those characters were originally modelled on the Zanucks and Hydes of Hollywood in the early fifties. Sergius' comment that he had gone to Desert D'Or 'because the people who manufactured images fascinated me'[22] could well stand as a comment on Mailer's attitude in *Marilyn*. His fascination with the very famous personalities of his time, rather like Scott Fitzgerald's fascination with the very rich, is an ambiguous mixture of distance and identification, criticism and admiration.

Very famous during her lifetime, since her death Monroe – along with James Dean and Bogart – has become one of the legendary cult figures of cinema. Mailer's book is both a contribution to the cult and a critique of it. Aside from its obvious appeal therefore *Marilyn* offers a glimpse of the cultural climate of the fifties and of the 'people who manufactured images' – images which had such a monumental effect on mass consciousness at that time. But apart from its popular appeal and the secondary sociological significance, as a novel *or* biography of Marilyn Monroe, the book is not successful. The substructure, the facts of her life based on Zolotow and Guiles, is overlaid with Mailer's 'theorisation' of the biographical details, and the facts and the theories, biography and novel for the most part fail to cohere.

Monroe's early life, her illegitimacy, her disturbed childhood, the family history of insanity and breakdown, provide the background to her psychological problems as an adult. The later strains of being turned into the world's biggest sex-symbol in Hollywood (which, as Mailer suggests here and in *The Deer Park*, can threaten the sanity of many a stronger personality) offer a perfectly adequate explanation of why at the age of thirty-six without close friends or a job, she committed suicide by an overdose of barbiturates. But while at one level Mailer accepts the obvious explanations, at another he forces his material into his own theses on mystery, magic and madness. 'Forces' because these attempted connections are frequently awkward, made with a self-conscious, defensive verbosity. Even when one accepts Mailer's basic project, his right to fictionalise that material, to invent dialogue and to 'look into the unspoken impulses of his real characters', it is difficult to accept the obtrusive voice of Norman Mailer making inflated claims, tactical qualifications and extended formulations of ideas well documented elsewhere. The difficulty is *not* with the novelist's imagination, but with the interventions of the dogmatic theorist too impatient to create imaginative connections between his ideas and his material.

The second chapter, 'Buried Alive', which deals with Norma Jean's family, is a fairly typical example of this method. After speculating about the identity of her father, his 'manhood' and the possibility that as a 'stud' his greatest gift to his daughter was 'libido', he comments that

> It is the acme of the facetious to speculate about the
> character of her father.[23]

He then goes on to explain why (in 1926) the pregnant mother
did not have an abortion with a teleological suggestion which
has a great deal to do with his own theories about procreation,
but little to do with Gladys Baker at that point:

> Some inner imperative may have told her that this child
> was too special to abort.

The fact, or 'factoid', that as a baby Norma Jean rarely cried is
seen as 'the first sign of the spiritual orphan who does not
expect attention'. Since Mailer later explains Monroe's exhibitionism in terms of her orphaned childhood, some further
comment is necessary – but missing. Again, after a sen-
sationalised description of the grandmother's attempt to
smother the one-year old child as a dialogue with eternity, he
adds,

> Of course, short of Marilyn's dubious witness, we do not
> know that Della ever touched the child.[25]

Alternately sentimental and melodramatic about Monroe as
'an angelic and sensitive victim or a murderous emotional crip-
ple'[26], Mailer exploits the most melodramatic of journalistic
factoids and then covers himself with disclaimers, apologies,
concessions to more realistic interpretations. This refusal to
take up any position towards the statements he offers, or at least
reproduces, robs the book of any coherence. There is an endless
succession of equivocations,

> Let us dare the argument that . . .
> One might well assume . . .
> we will hardly know for certain . . .
> we can pick up the hint that . . .
> We draw back from such a projection . . .
> It is conceivable that . . .
> It is worth supposing that . . .
> If such a notion has value, let us assume that . . .
> Let us assume it even happened in some fashion . . .[27]

a style filled with 'probably', 'perhaps', 'of course' and 'in fact' testifies to Mailer's lack of conviction as a biographer and novelist. Having claimed the 'sanction' of the novelist to invent and create, he relies not on the authority of his imagination, but on legalistic sophistries.

Dealing with Monroe's death at the end of the book, the author spends several pages speculating on the fact that the autopsy showed her stomach and intestines were empty. The murder theory is considered and the involvement of the FBI, the CIA, the Mafia and the Kennedy family are ponderously weighed. Then Mailer devalues all that has gone before by protecting himself, legally and intellectually, with the following statement:

> There seems next to nothing of such evidence, and we have all the counterproof of Marilyn's instablity, and the real likelihood that she had taken too many barbiturates . . .[28]

The fixity of the more realistic explanation does not, however, fit his need for a dramatic ending, so he returns to calling it a 'mystery';

> We will never know if that is how she went. She could as easily have blundered past the last border, blubbering in the last corner of her heart. She came to us in all her mother's doubt and leaves in mystery.[29]

Thus Mailer's dualistic habits triumph over the challenge of the new genre and the complexities of his subject's character. Having characterised her as a schizophrenic angel-beast, turned the obscurity of her birth into a 'mystery', he inflates the amibiguities of her death into another. Where the material will not easily divide into his dichotomies, he becomes mystical about the difficulties of doing so. As Poirier says of his method in *A Fire on the Moon*,

> Divide the material, argue the differences, reach a kind of stalemate and call it a 'mystery'.

The book ends on a note of fulsome whimsy and an echo of Rojack's goodbye to Cherry:

> Let her be rather in one place and not scattered in pieces

across the firmament; let us hope her mighty soul and the mouse of her little one are both recovering their proportions in some fair and gracious home, and she will soon return to us from retirement. It is the devil of her humor and the curse of our land that she will come back speaking Chinese. Goodbye Norma Jean. Au revoir Marilyn. When you happen on Bobby and Jack, give them the wink. And if there's a wish, pay your visit to Mr. Dickens. For he, like many another literary man, is bound to adore you, fatherless child.[30]

The inadequacies of *Marilyn*, it seems to me, relate once more to Mailer's problems with voice. In *The Armies of the Night* Mailer bridged the novel-history distinction and the problem of authorial voice by turning himself into a novelistic character called 'Norman Mailer'. This creation gave him a subjective vantage-point from which to expound his ideas while, at the same time, forcing a new objectivity into the self-presentation. In *Marilyn* the authorial voice is partially objectified into 'the novelist' and 'the new candidate for biographer', but generally the author's voice (insistently present throughout) is not integrated with the other material. Exceptionally, there are passages where his comments and generalisations are fully and effectively connected with the biographical themes; the passages describing the masculine world of sportsmen and Monroe's uneasy role as 'queen of the working-class' while married to Joe DiMaggio, work as general social observation but also provide the 'setting' for the failure of their relationship. Similarly, the capsule reviews of Hollywood films and the plays of Tennesse Williams and Arthur Miller serve to suggest some of the contradictions in the culture in which Monroe lived and worked. Mailer's sexual and literary rivalry with Miller, on the other hand, is developed beyond any need of story or setting and at times actually obscures Miller's relations with Marilyn. (In *The Armies of the Night* Mailer's personal attitudes toward Lowell or Dwight Macdonald are described as those of one 'fictional' character to another, and further, Norman Mailer is exposed to *their* scrutiny.) Behind the Arthur Miller who is described as 'this tall and timid hero of middle-class life', we imagine a small, bold, middle-class villain called Norman

Mailer. The reader is invited to do this, because the authorial voice directs his sympathies away from Miller – *not* towards Monroe – but towards a character who dominates every chapter, but who never emerges from the twilight world of the novel-biography.

The paradox is that Mailer's gifts are those of an imaginative writer, a novelist, but that he is a writer who cannot, seemingly, entrust his ideas to fictional form – to his characters, narratives and settings. There are personal reasons for this, undoubtedly. In his case, the publishing battles of the fifties shook his faith not just in publishing but in the kind of work he had up until then been producing. The shift into the first person was directly correlated with that experience. But the experience (and not just Mailer's reaction to it) raises social and aesthetic questions which all contemporary novelists have to face. This book is mainly concerned with Mailer's achievements and technical problems – and as an interim study is necessarily tentative and provisional in its conclusions – but a more definitive assessment would have to locate his work in a general analysis of the contemporary novel.

The central idea of his writings is one of the characteristic ideas of this century – the assertion and preservation of individuality during a time of great changes in the structure of society. His attempt to write about those changes and to defend what he feels is in danger, has led him to abandon traditional forms. Like Sam Slovoda, he might perhaps wish to write a realistic novel but since 'reality is no longer realistic' – at least in the nineteenth-century sense – must devise new methods to describe contemporary, 'non-realistic' reality. And although some novelists have been able to use the known forms (often, in England, at the cost of excluding important new experiences), almost *all* contemporary writers are engaged in a search for forms which can adequately express their perception of a changing world. It is important, therefore, to situate Mailer's endeavours and failures in in this context. However unsatisfactory some of his experiments are, I think he is right to make such attempts. New acts of perception, interpretation and organisation are necessary for literature at the moment. Developments in the communications field – television as surely as the invention of the printing press – force literature into radically new relationships and forms. The problem with Mailer is not simply to separate the artist from the propagandist and to narrow his social theories down to a few 'timeless' literary truths. Nor is the intellectual quality of his theories of paramount importance, since many writers – Yeats is an obvious example – have produced new and excellent literature, based on equally dubious thought-systems. His real problem, I think, is not to jettison his ideas, or abandon fiction for journalism, but to redefine the *relation* between his art and his ideas and to accept the specific long-term effectiveness of fiction as a means of changing people's consciousness.

Notes

INTRODUCTION

1 *The Armies of the Night*, p. 185
2 *Advertisements for Myself*, p. 307
3 *Cannibals and Christians*, p. 125
4 Ibid., p. 125
5 *Advertisements for Myself*, p. 17

1 'THE BEAST AND THE SEER'

1 *The Naked and the Dead*, p. 189
2 Ibid., p. 244
3 Ibid., p. 314
4 Ibid., p. 423
5 Ibid., p. 314
6 Ibid., p. 36
7 Ibid., p. 374
8 Ibid., p. 102
9 Ibid., p. 245
10 Ibid., pp. 245–6
11 Ibid., p. 435
12 Ibid., p. 66
13 Ibid., p. 248
14 Ibid., p. 158
15 Ibid., p. 431
16 Ibid., p. 20
17 Ibid., p. 39
18 Ibid., p. 105
19 Ibid., p. 87
20 Ibid., p. 228
21 Ibid., p. 467
22 Ibid., p. 79
23 Ibid., p. 79
24 Ibid., p. 79
25 Ibid., p. 465

26 Ibid., p. 465
27 Ibid.
28 Ibid., p. 468
29 Ibid., p. 502
30 Ibid., p. 509
31 Ibid., p. 499
32 Ibid., p. 504
33 Ibid., p. 503
34 Ibid., p. 510
35 Ibid., p. 511
36 Ibid., p. 527
37 *Advertisements for Myself*, p. 87
38 *Barbary Shore*, p. 191
39 Ibid., p. 286
40 Ibid., p. 283
41 Ibid., p. 261
42 Ibid., p. 116
43 Ibid., p. 221
44 Ibid., p. 152
45 *Advertisements for Myself*, p. 98
46 *The Deer Park*, p. 56
47 Ibid., p. 56
48 Ibid., p. 83
49 *Advertisements for Myself*, p. 204
50 *The Deer Park*, p. 13
51 Ibid., p. 56
52 Ibid., p. 13
53 Ibid., p. 388
54 Ibid., p. 194
55 Ibid., p. 157
56 Ibid., p. 170
57 Ibid., p. 157
58 Ibid., p. 354
59 Ibid., p. 171
60 Ibid., p. 340
61 Ibid., p. 388
62 Ibid., p. 41
63 Ibid., p. 42
64 Ibid., p. 41
65 Ibid., p. 53
66 Ibid., p. 190
67 Ibid., p. 381
68 Ibid., p. 112
69 Ibid., p. 133
70 Ibid., p. 180
71 Ibid., p. 119
72 Ibid., p. 212
73 Ibid., p. 269

74 Ibid., p. 213
75 Ibid., p. 192
76 Ibid., p. 65
77 Ibid., p. 133
78 Ibid., p. 239
79 *Advertisements for Myself*, p. 272
80 Ibid., p. 283 (My italics)
81 Ibid., p. 170
82 Ibid., p. 283
83 Ibid., p. 285
84 Ibid., p. 309
85 Ibid., p. 310
86 *The Presidential Papers*, p. 212
87 Ibid., p. 54
88 Ibid., p. 58
89 Ibid., p. 58
90 Ibid., p. 16
91 Ibid., p. 17
92 Ibid., p. 52
93 Ibid., p. 55
94 Ibid., p. 12
95 Ibid., p. 11
96 Ibid., p. 51
97 Ibid., p. 50
98 Ibid., p. 68
99 Ibid., p. 166
100 *An American Dream*, p. 14
101 Ibid., p. 15
102 Ibid., p. 10
103 Ibid., p. 122
104 Ibid., p. 12
105 Ibid., p. 15
106 Ibid., p. 23
107 Ibid., p. 24
108 Ibid., p. 43
109 Ibid., p. 36
110 Ibid., p. 36
111 Ibid., p. 35
112 Ibid., p. 194
113 Ibid., p. 191
114 Ibid., p. 185
115 Ibid., p. 251
116 Ibid., p. 251
117 Ibid., p. 36
118 *Why are We in Vietnam?*, p. 203
119 Ibid., p. 150
120 Ibid., p. 34
121 Ibid., p. 152

122 Ibid., p. 175
123 Ibid., p. 203
124 Ibid., p. 8
125 Ibid., p. 174
126 *Go Down Moses* (Penguin, Harmondsworth, 1960) p. 158
127 *Why are We in Vietnam?*, p. 54
128 Ibid., p. 60
129 Ibid., p. 175
130 Ibid., p. 188
131 Ibid., pp. 203–4
132 Ibid., p. 8
133 Ibid., p. 9
134 *Cannibals and Christians*, p. 71
135 See Mailer's comments on the language of *Why are We in Vietnam?* in *The Armies of the Night*, p. 48
136 *Cannibals and Christians*, p. 126

2 'A REVOLUTION IN THE CONSCIOUSNESS OF OUR TIME'

1 *The Armies of the Night*, p. 25
2 *Advertisements for Myself*, p. 26
3 *The Naked and the Dead*, p. 136
4 *The Naked and the Dead*, p. 212
5 Ibid., p. 246
6 Ibid., p. 68
7 Ibid., p. 27
8 Ibid., p. 244
9 Ibid., p. 429
10 Ibid., p. 320
11 Ibid., p. 537
12 Ibid., p. 584
13 Ibid., p. 537
14 *Barbary Shore*, p. 11
15 Ibid., p. 121
16 Ibid., p. 121
17 Ibid., p. 286
18 Ibid., p. 271
19 Ibid., p. 285
20 Ibid., p. 33
21 Ibid., p. 235
22 Ibid., pp. 191–2
23 *Advertisements for Myself*, p. 88
24 See Daniel Bell, *The End of Ideology* (New York, 1960), Chapter 14 and the epilogue
25 *Advertisements for Myself*, p. 230 (My italics)
26 *The Deer Park*, p. 10
27 *Advertisements for Myself*, p. 204

28 *The Deer Park*, p. 34
29 Ibid., p. 316
30 Ibid., p. 379
31 Ibid., p. 381
32 *Advertisements for Myself*, p. 271
33 Ibid., p. 23
34 H. Arendt, *Origins of Totalitarianism* (London, 1958)
35 *Advertisements for Myself*, pp. 293–4
36 Ibid., p. 293
37 N. Podhoretz, 'Norman Mailer: The Embattled Vision', *Partisan Review* (Summer 1959); J. Baldwin, *Nobody Knows My Name* (New York, 1962)
38 *Advertisements for Myself*, p. 151
39 Ibid., p. 163
40 Ibid., p. 163
41 *Cannibals and Christians*, p. 105
42 *Advertisements for Myself*, p. 17
43 *The Presidential Papers*, p. 11
44 *Cannibals and Christians*, p. 43
45 *The Presidential Papers*, p. 17
46 *Cannibals and Christians*, p. 200
47 *The Presidential Papers*, p. 201
48 *Cannibals and Christians*, p. 72
49 *The Presidential Papers*, p. 89
50 Ibid., p. 82
51 Ibid., p. 85
52 Ibid., p. 85
53 Ibid., p. 139
54 *Advertisements for Myself*, p. 86
55 *The Presidential Papers*, p. 140
56 Ibid., p. 140
57 *Cannibals and Christians*, p. 31
58 Ibid., p. 42
59 Ibid., p. 42
60 *Miami and the Siege of Chicago*, p. 52
61 *Miami and the Siege of Chicago*, p. 184
62 *The Armies of the Night*, p. 9
63 Ibid., p. 9
64 Ibid., p. 63
65 Ibid., p. 118
66 Ibid., p. 118
67 Ibid., p. 88
68 Ibid., p. 87
69 Ibid., p. 88
70 Ibid., p. 179
71 *Miami and the Siege of Chicago*, p. 182
72 *The Prisoner of Sex*, p. 222

3 'THE BEST WRITER IN AMERICA'

1 *Advertisements for Myself*, p. 26
2 Ibid., p. 63
3 *The Naked and the Dead*, p. 171
4 Ibid., p. 173
5 *Writers at Work*, III
6 Ibid., p. 261
7 Cited above, p. 7
8 Cited above, p. 7
9 *The Naked and the Dead*, p. 337
10 Ibid., p. 120
11 *Barbary Shore*, p. 9
12 *Advertisements for Myself*, pp. 78–9
13 *Writers at Work*, III 262
14 Ibid., p. 263
15 *Barbary Shore*, p. 11
16 *Advertisements for Myself*, p. 88
17 *The Deer Park*, p. 388
18 Ibid., p. 171
19 Ibid., p. 215
20 Ibid., p. 318
21 Ibid., p. 387
22 *Advertisements for Myself*, p. 203
23 *The Deer Park*, p. 100
24 Ibid., p. 327
25 *Barbary Shore*, p. 16
26 *The Deer Park*, p. 369
27 Ibid., p. 369
28 *Advertisements for Myself*, p. 17
29 Ibid., p. 187
30 Ibid., p. 199
31 Ibid., p. 201
32 Interview in *The New Yorker* (23 Oct 1948)
33 *Advertisements for Myself*, p. 21
34 Ibid., p. 87
35 Ibid., p. 148
36 Ibid., p. 166
37 Ibid., p. 171
38 Ibid., p. 293
39 Ibid., p. 271
40 Ibid., p. 425
41 Ibid., p. 430
42 Ibid., p. 423
43 *Cannibals and Christians*, p. 383
44 Ibid., p. 251
45 Ibid., p. 92
46 Ibid., p. 201

47 Ibid., p. 94
48 Ibid., p. 94
49 Ibid., p. 103
50 Ibid., p. 105
51 Ibid., p. 105
52 *Why are We in Vietnam?*, p. 22
53 Ibid., p. 34
54 Ibid., p. 33
55 Ibid., pp. 24–5
56 *Cannibals and Christians*, p. 71
57 *Why are We in Vietnam?*, p. 8
58 Ibid., p. 7
59 Ibid., p. 9
60 Elizabeth Hardwick, 'Bad Boy', *Partisan Review* (Mar 1965)
61 *An American Dream*, p. 49
62 Ibid., p. 52
63 Ibid., p. 58
64 Ibid., p. 123
65 Ibid., pp. 122–3
66 Ibid., p. 133
67 Ibid., p. 136
68 Ibid., p. 136
69 Tony Tanner, 'On the Parapet', *The Critical Quarterly* (Summer 1970)
70 *An American Dream*, p. 10
71 *The Presidential Papers*, p. 200
72 *An American Dream*, p. 9
73 Ibid., p. 223
74 Ibid., p. 23
75 Ibid., p. 153
76 Ibid., p. 10
77 Ibid., p. 40
78 Ibid., p. 10
79 Ibid., p. 238
80 *Advertisements for Myself*, p. 203
81 Ibid., p. 204
82 Sartre's phrase in his essay, 'Francois Mauriac and Freedom', *Literary &*
     Philosophical Essays (London, 1955)
83 *Advertisements for Myself*, p. 399
84 Sartre, 'Francois Mauriac and Freedom'
85 *Cannibals and Christians*, p. 245
86 Ibid., p. 410
87 Ibid., p. 349
88 Ibid., p. 383
89 Ibid., p 410
90 *Why are We in Vietnam?*, p. 150
91 Ibid., p. 24
92 Ibid., p. 134
93 Ibid., p. 208

94 Ibid., p. 23
95 Ibid., p. 14
96 *An American Dream*, p. 179
97 *The Armies of the Night*, p. 255
98 Ibid., p. 255
99 Ibid., p. 256
100 Ibid., p. 257
101 Ibid., p. 9
102 *The Presidential Papers*, p. 125
103 *The Armies of the Night*, p. 22
104 Ibid., p. 157
105 Ibid.
106 Ibid., p. 255
107 *The Prisoner of Sex*, p. 233

4 'THE PRISONER OF SEX'

1 *The Prisoner of Sex*, p. 45
2 *The Naked and the Dead*, p. 144
3 Ibid., p. 196
4 Ibid., p. 197
5 Ibid., p. 196
6 Ibid., p. 49
7 Ibid., p. 127
8 Ibid., p. 144
9 Ibid., p. 57
10 Ibid., p. 56
11 Ibid., p. 48
12 Ibid., p. 48
13 Ibid., p. 213
14 Ibid., p. 217
15 Ibid., p. 245
16 Ibid., p. 127
17 Ibid., p. 314
18 Ibid., p. 123
19 Ibid., p. 125
20 Ibid., p. 428
21 *The Presidential Papers*, p. 149
22 *Barbary Shore*, p. 149
23 Ibid., p. 19
24 Ibid., p. 279
25 Ibid., p. 22
26 Ibid., p. 132
27 Ibid., p. 64
28 Ibid., p. 64
29 *Advertisements for Myself*, p. 190

30 *Advertisements for Myself*, p. 228
31 *The Deer Park*, p. 10
32 Ibid., p. 12
33 Ibid., p. 15
34 Ibid., p. 56
35 Ibid., p. 93
36 *Barbary Shore*, p. 64
37 *The Deer Park*, p. 103
38 Ibid., p. 140
39 Ibid., p. 139
40 Ibid., p. 131
41 *Advertisements for Myself*, p. 204
42 *The Deer Park*, p. 250
43 Ibid., p. 269
44 Kate Millett, *Sexual Politics* (New York, 1970) p. 318
45 *The Deer Park*, p. 385
46 Ibid., p. 25
47 Ibid., p. 119
48 Ibid., p. 165
49 *Advertisements for Myself*, p. 272
50 Ibid., p. 390
51 Ibid., p. 148
52 Ibid., p. 147
53 Ibid., p. 163
54 In the list of hip-square oppositions on pp. 346–8 in *Advertisements for Myself*, Mailer calls 'sex for orgasm' hip and 'sex for ego' the square equivalent
55 *Advertisements for Myself*, p. 403
56 Ibid., p. 271
57 Ibid., p. 283
58 D. H. Lawrence, *Lady Chatterley's Lover* (Florence, 1928) p. 316
59 *The Presidential Papers*, p. 143
60 Ibid., p. 151
61 Ibid., p. 157
62 *The Presidential Papers*, p. 114
63 Ibid., p. 140
64 *Cannibals and Christians*, p. 255
65 *An American Dream*, p. 12
66 Richard Poirier, 'Morbid-Mindedness', *Commentary* (June 1964)
67 *An American Dream*, p. 192
68 Ibid., p. 196
69 Ibid., p. 43
70 Ibid., p. 16
71 Ibid., p. 36
72 Ibid., p. 45
73 Ibid., p. 52
74 Ibid., p. 124
75 *The Prisoner of Sex*, p. 43

76 Ibid., pp. 49–50
77 Ibid., p. 71
78 Ibid., p. 80
79 Ibid., pp. 186–7
80 Ibid., p. 97. The 'sawn-off shotgun' is of course the weapon used by those
    hunters in *Why are We in Vietnam?* who practice an inauthentic violence
    against nature and the animals in Brooks Range
81 Ibid., p. 45
82 Ibid., p. 60
83 Ibid., p. 110
84 Ibid., p. 44
85 Ibid., p. 62
86 Ibid., p. 231
87 Ibid., p. 223
88 Ibid., p. 39

CONCLUSION

1 *Advertisements for Myself*, p. 201
2 Ibid., p. 201
3 *The Deer Park*, p. 388
4 *Advertisements for Myself*, p. 309
5 Ibid., p. 309
6 Robert A. Bone, 'Private Mailer Re-enlists', *Dissent* (Autumn 1960)
7 Millett, *Sexual Politics*, p. 315
8 *Cannibals and Christians*, pp. 413–14
9 Ibid., p. 258
10 *A Fire on the Moon*, p. 5
11 John Berger, 'The Political Uses of Photo-Montage', *New Society* (23 Oct
    1969)
12 *The Prisoner of Sex*, p. 22
13 Richard Poirier, *Mailer* (London, 1972) p. 11

EPILOGUE

1 *St George*, p.3
2 Ibid., p.6
3 Ibid., p. 155
4 Ibid., p. 56
5 Ibid., p. 57
6 Ibid., p. 93
7 Ibid., p. 178
8 Ibid., p. 204
9 Ibid., p. 179
10 Ibid., p.106
11 Ibid., p. 173
12 Ibid., p. 31
13 *The Armies of the Night*, p. 22

14 *Existential Errands*, p. xi
15 *The Presidential Papers*, p. 231 or p. 261
16 *Existential Errands*, p. 17
17 Ibid., p. 17
18 Ibid., p. 26
19 Ibid., p. 33
20 Ibid., p. 100
21 *Marilyn*, p. 20
22 *The Deer Park* (Play) p. 155
23 *Marilyn*, p. 25
24 Ibid, p. 26
25 Ibid., p. 29
26 Ibid, p. 23
27 Ibid., all from chapter 2, 'Buried Alive!'
28 Ibid., p. 244
29 Ibid.
30 Ibid., p. 248

Selected Bibliography

WORKS BY MAILER

The Naked and the Dead (New York: Rinehart, 1948).

Barbary Shore (New York: Rinehart, 1951).

The Deer Park (New York: Putnam's, 1955).

Advertisements for Myself (New York: Putnam's, 1959).

Deaths for the Ladies (and other Disasters) (New York: Putnam's, 1962).

The Presidential Papers (New York: Putnam's, 1963).

An American Dream (New York: The Dial Press, 1965). (Originally appeared in monthly instalments in *Esquire* (Jan –Aug 1964).)

Cannibals and Christians (New York: The Dial Press, 1966).

The Deer Park, a Play (New York: The Dial Press, 1967).

Why are We in Vietnam? (New York: Putnam's, 1967).

The Armies of the Night (New York: New American Library, 1968).

Miami and the Siege of Chicago (New York: New American Library, 1968).

A Fire on the Moon (Boston: Little, Brown, 1970).

The Prisoner of Sex (Boston: Little, Brown, 1971).

On the Fight of the Century: King of the Hill (New York: Signet Paperback, 1971).

St. George and the Godfather (New York: New American Library, 1972).

Existential Errands (New York: New American Library, 1973).

Marilyn (New York: Grosset & Dunlap, 1973).

CRITICAL MATERIAL

In Books

Aldridge, John W., *After the Lost Generation* (New York, 1951).

Baldwin, James, *Nobody Knows My Name* (New York, 1962).

Bergonzi, Bernard, *The Situation of the Novel* (London, 1970).

Blotner, Joseph, *The Modern American Political Novel* (University of Texas, 1966).

Current Biography (New York, 1948).

Eisinger, Chester E, *Fiction of the Forties* (University of Chicago, 1963).

Ellman, Mary, *Thinking about Women* (New York, 1968).

Fiedler, Leslie A., *Waiting for the End* (London, 1964).

Flaherty, Joe, *Managing Mailer* (New York, 1970).

Foster, Richard, *Norman Mailer* (University of Minnesota pamphlet, 1968).

Geismar, Maxwell, *American Moderns* (New York, 1958).

Greer, Germaine, *The Female Eunuch* (London, 1971).

Harper, Howard M., *Desperate Faith* (University of North Carolina, 1967).

Hassan, Ihab, *Radical Innocence* (Princeton, New Jersey, 1961).

Hoffman, Frederick, *The Modern Novel in America* (Chicago, 1951).

Howe, Irving, *A World More Attractive* (New York, 1963).

Kaufman, Donald L., *Norman Mailer: The Countdown* (Southern Illinois University Press, 1969).

Kazin, Alfred, *Contemporaries* (Boston, 1962).

Lasch, Christopher, *The New Radicalism in America, 1889–1963* (New York, 1965).

Leeds, Barry M., *The Structured Vision of Norman Mailer* (New York, 1969).

Millett, Kate, *Sexual Politics* (New York, 1970).

Millgate, Michael, *American Social Fiction* (New York, 1964).

Podhoretz, Norman, *Doings and Undoings* (New York, 1964).

Poirier, Richard, *Mailer* (London, 1972).

Rideout, Walter B., *The Radical Novel in the United States, 1900–1954* (Cambridge, Mass. 1956).

Tanner, Tony, *City of Words* (New York, 1971).

Trilling, Diana, *Claremont Essays* (New York, 1964).

Waldmeir, Joseph J., *American Novels of the Second World War* (Paris, 1969).

In Periodicals

Aldridge, John W., 'Victim and Analyst', *Commentary* (Mar 1966).

——, 'From Vietnam to Obscurity', *Harpers* (Jul 1967).

Alvarez, A., 'Norman X', *Spectator* (7 May 1965).

——, 'Art and Isolation', *Listener* (1957).

Beaver, Harold, 'A Figure in the Carpet: Irony and the American Novel', *Essays and Studies*, xv (1962).

Bersani, Leo, 'The Interpretation of Dreams', *Partisan Review*, xxxii (Fall 1965).

Bone, Robert A., 'Private Mailer Re-enlists', *Dissent* (Autumn 1960).

Bryant, Jerry H., 'The Last of the Social Protest Writers', *Arizona Quarterly* (Winter 1963).

Chase, Richard, 'Novelist Going Places', *Commentary* (Dec 1955).

Corrington, John W., 'An American Dreamer', *Chicago Review* (1965).

Cowley, Malcolm, 'The Literary Situation', *University of Mississippi Studies in English* (1965).

De Mott, B., 'Docket No. 15883', *American Scholar* (Spring 1961).

Dupee, F. W., 'American Norman Mailer', *Commentary* (Feb 1960).

Epstein, Joseph, 'Norman Mailer: The Literary Man's Cassius Clay', *New Republic* (17 Apr 1965).

Fitch, R. E., 'Mystique de la merde', *New Republic* (3 Sep 1956).

Gilman, Richard, 'Why Mailer wants to be President', *New Republic* (8 Feb 1964).

——, 'What Mailer has done', *New Republic* (8 Jun 1968).

Glicksberg, Charles I., 'Norman Mailer: Angry Young Novelist in America', *Wisconsin Studies* (Winter 1960).

Goldman, Lawrence, 'The Political Vision of Norman Mailer', *Studies on the Left* (Summer 1964).

Greedfeld, J., 'Line Between Literature and Journalism Thin But', *Commonweal* (Jun 1968).

Hampshire, Stuart, 'Mailer United', *New Statesman* (13 Oct 1961).

Hardwick, Elizabeth, 'Bad Boy', *Partisan Review* (Mar 1965).

Hassan, Ihab, 'The Way Down and Out', *Virginia Quarterly* (Winter 1963).

Hoffman, Frederick J., 'Norman Mailer and the Revolt of the Ego: Some Observations on Recent American Literature', *Wisconsin Studies* (Autumn 1961).

Jones, James, 'Small Comment from a Penitent Novelist', *Esquire* (Dec 1968).

Kael, P., 'Imagination and the Age', *Reporter* (1 Oct 1966).

Kazin, Alfred, 'The Jew as a Modern Writer', *Commentary* (Apr 1966).

Kermode, Frank, 'Rammel', *New Statesman* (14 May 1965).

Krim, Seymour, 'A Hungry Mental Lion', *Evergreen Review* (Jan –Feb 1960).

Lakin, R. D., 'The Displaced Writer in America', *Midwest Quarterly* (Summer 1963).

Langbaum, Robert, 'Mailer's New Style', *Novel*, No. 2 (1968–9).

Lodge, David, 'Novelist at the Crossroads', *Critical Quarterly* (Summer 1969).

MacDonald, Dwight, 'Art, Life and Violence', *Commentary* (Jun 1962).

——, 'Our Far-Flung Correspondents', *New Yorker* (8 Oct 1960).

Mudrick, Marvin, Interview, *New Yorker* (23 Oct 1948).

——, 'Mailer and Styron: Guests of the Establishment', *Hudson Review* (Autumn 1964).

Poirier, Richard, 'Morbid-Mindedness', *Commentary* (Jun 1965).

Rahv, Philip, 'Crime Without Punishment', *New York Review of Books* (25 Mar 1965).

Richardson, Jack, 'The Aesthetics of Norman Mailer', *New York Review of Books* (8 May 1969).

Richler, Mordecai, 'Rugged Times', *New Yorker* (23 Oct 1948).

——, 'Norman Mailer', *Encounter* (Jul 1965).

Sale, Roger, 'Watchman, What of the Night?', *New York Review of Books* (6 May 1971).

Shrader, G. A., 'Norman Mailer and the Despair of Defiance', *Yale Review* (Winter 1962).

Solotaroff, Richard, 'Down Mailer's Way', *Chicago Review* (Fall 1966).

Steiner, George, 'Naked but not Dead', *Encounter* (Dec 1961).

Swados, Harvey, 'Must Writers be Characters?', *Saturday Review* (1 Oct 1960).

Thompson, John, 'Catching up on Mailer', *New York Review of Books* (20 Apr 1967).

Time Magazine, 'Norman's Phantasmagoria', (15 Nov 1971).

Toback, James, 'Norman Mailer Today', *Commentary* (Oct 1967).

Velde, R., 'Hemingway Who Stayed Home', *Nation* (20 Jan 1964).

Vidal, Gore, 'The Norman Mailer Syndrome', *Nation* (2 Jan 1960).

Wagenheim, Allen J., 'Square's Progress: An American Dream', *Critique*, 10, No. 1 (1968).

Waldmeir, Joseph J., 'Accommodations in the New Novel', *University College Quarterly* (Nov 1965).

Weber, Brom, 'A Fear of Dying', *Hollins Critic*, ii, iii (1965).

ADDITIONAL MATERIAL

Arendt, Hannah, *Origins of Totalitarianism*, 2nd enl. ed. of 'The Burden of our Time' (London, 1958).

Baldwin, James, *Another Country* (London, 1963).

Bell, Daniel, *The End of Ideology* (New York, 1960).

Blackham, H. J., *Six Existentialist Thinkers* (London, 1952).

Brown, Norman O., *Life Against Death* (London, 1959).

——, *Love's Body* (New York, 1966).

Carlyle, Thomas, *Sartor Resartus; Heroes and Hero-Worship, Past and Present; The French Revolution* (London, 1857).

Chomsky, Noam, 'The Responsibility of Intellectuals', in *The Dissenting Academy*, ed. Theodore Roszak (New York, 1967).

Cozzens, James Gould, *Guard of Honour* (London, 1949).

Dawson, Victoria, 'Contrasting Attitudes to War and American Society between 1920–1961 in the Works of Dos Passos and Norman Mailer', London University M. A. thesis, 1965.

Dissent, 1954–1970, especially vols. ii, iii, iv, v, and vi.

Faulkner, William, 'The Bear', in *Go Down Moses* (New York, 1942).

Fitzgerald, F. Scott, *The Great Gatsby* (date 1925), *Tender is the Night* (date 1934), *The Last Tycoon* (date 1941).

Goodman, Paul, *Growing Up Absurd* (London, 1961).

——, *Utopian Essays and Practical Proposals* (New York, 1962).

Howe, Irving, *Politics and the Novel* (New York, 1957).

———, *William Faulkner* (New York, 1952).

Koestler, Arthur, *Darkness at Noon* (London, 1940).

Lerner, Max, *America as a Civilisation* (London, 1958).

Lukacs, Georg, *The Meaning of Contemporary Realism* (London, 1963).

MacDonald, Dwight, *Against the American Grain* (London, 1963).

Malin, Irving, *Jews and Americans* (Southern Illinois University Press, 1965).

Malraux, André, *Man's Fate* (London, 1948).

Mannheim, Karl, *Ideology and Utopia* (London, 1936).

Orwell, George, *1984* (London, 1948).

Podhoretz, Norman, *Making It* (New York, 1967).

Reich, Wilhelm, *Discovery of the Orgone* (New York, 1942).

———, *The Sexual Revolution* (New York, 1945).

———, *Mass Psychology of Fascism* (New York, 1946).

Sartre, J. P., *Literary and Philosophical Essays* (London, 1955).

Serge, Victor, *From Lenin to Stalin* (London, 1937).

Shaw, Irwin, *The Young Lions* (New York, 1948).

Sontag, Susan, *Against Interpretation* (New York, 1967).

Teodori, Massimo (ed.), *The New Left: A Documentary History* (New York, 1969).

Trotsky, Leon, *The New Course* (New York, 1943).

West, Mathanael, *Miss Lonelyhearts* (New York, 1933).

Williams, Raymond, *Culture and Society* (London, 1958).

Woolf, Cecil and John Baguley (eds.), *Authors Take Sides on Vietnam* (London, 1967).

Wouk, Herman, *The Caine Mutiny* (New York, 1951).

Index

201